PARTNERSHIP FOR PROGRESS

PARTNERSHIP FOR PROGRESS

A Program for Transatlantic Action

By Pierre Uri
DIRECTOR OF STUDIES OF THE ATLANTIC INSTITUTE

Preface by Henry Cabot Lodge
DIRECTOR-GENERAL OF THE ATLANTIC INSTITUTE

English edition by William J. Miller

PUBLISHED FOR THE ATLANTIC INSTITUTE BY

Harper & Row, Publishers

NEW YORK AND EVANSTON

Project manager and research: Marc Ullmann

CONTENTS

PREFACE

T<small>HE</small> Atlantic Institute has been looking at the way in which that part of the world which is definitely not Communist is organized. And we are brought to this conclusion: that the non-Communist world is in disorder—and that many are complacent about it. This is not to belittle existing international organizations, all of which are indispensable in various ways and are a credit to those who created them. But none of them even pretend to organize the non-Communists on a world-wide basis and the sum total of them has thus not made our free world "operational."

There is no lack of excellent statements of the truth that the nations of the free world are interdependent. Even the most chauvinistic do not deny that the well-being of every nation— even that of the United States—will depend increasingly on its participation in some sort of grouping of nations and that none can cope with today's problems alone. There is thus a widespread demand in the Atlantic world for more teamwork. But when it comes to doing something concrete and practical to give effect to these ideals, the results are inadequate.

Our failure to organize ourselves is certainly not due to any lack of warning. As far back as 1958 the Rockefeller Brothers Fund Report said: "The free world must devise the institutions for a world community in which free societies may flourish and free men have the opportunity to realize their potentialities as human beings."

President Kennedy on July 4, 1962, in Independence Hall, said that "alone" the United States could do none of the big things which should be done in the world, but that "joined with other free nations" it could. He has acted in this spirit and Congress, in harmony with this attitude, has voted the Trade Expansion Act.

But, in contrast with these wise assertions and actions, what in 1963 do we actually see?

We see a free world which is strangling in its own tariff regulations and other red tape.

We see such a hopeful development as the European Common Market under a cloud.

We see an actual desire in some quarters to shrink still further the number of free nations which are grouped together, although the evidence underscores the need for organizing ever wider areas of land and ever larger numbers of people.

We see United States and European agriculture unable to devise joint means to use their surpluses and actually throwing up tariff barriers against each other's products.

We see a free world currency system which is so unstable that if the United States were required to assume substantially larger overseas financial obligations or if there were a run on British sterling, the result could be free world economic collapse.

We see uneven economic growth in the free world—with some nations going ahead and some stagnating. Indeed, the economies of some nations are so weak that they are an open invitation to Soviet domination.

On the other hand, we learn from Eastern Europe that there is a strong desire to develop a new relationship with the West which might conceivably bring results—*if* we were organized so that there would be something *to* which they could turn.

Hovering over the whole disorderly scene are the under-developed countries, which view the Common Market as it stands with grave misgivings, and which suspect that deals are being made at their expense under cover of the Common Market. Yet obviously the Common Market must not imply a withdrawal of the economically sophisticated peoples from a world in which economic and social conditions which have been taken for granted for centuries now seem intolerable. On the contrary, it would—and it should—be at the service of humanity.

These are all grave charges, but we believe they cannot be disproved.

And these charges do not take into account the threat of the Soviet economic offensive, with its dumping of oil, and the confusion in NATO—two major problems which are outside the scope of this report.

Yet there is, almost under our very noses, a clue as to how the free world could be more effectively arrayed. This clue is the completely new approach to international problems which was invented in Europe twelve years ago, when the Coal and Steel Community was created, whereby everything to do with coal and steel in Europe was treated as a whole regardless of national boundaries. This was followed by the creation of the European Atomic Energy Agency, which handles atomic matters regardless of frontiers. And out of the Messina Conference came the European Common Market, which is now creating a single great European market which may well surpass in size the purchasing power of the great free-trade area of the United States.

This approach consists in treating differences between nations as problems of common concern to be solved jointly—and imaginatively—and not as issues to be haggled over. And this approach also aims at accomplishing something concrete and practical which can be started now rather than something transcendental.

It is against this background that the Atlantic Institute publishes its first report—*Partnership for Progress: A Program for Transatlantic Action.*

And now the Allies, so recently united for their very survival in a grim and trying war, are in such glaring and hostile disorder that those who had even dared hope for some eventual form of political union hear, instead, a gloomsayer's prophecy that the Allies will "remain suspicious and distrustful of each other" and "disunited . . . till the end of time."

One might easily think that these words describe 1963 and the pall which has recently spread over hopes for a growing Atlantic Community. But the words just quoted were uttered in 1787 and described America's own thirteen original states. Only four years after they had won their independence, trade had well-nigh stopped among them, mutual confidence seemed totally lacking, and trade disputes were even threatening war among New York, Connecticut and New Jersey. New York was protecting its fuel interests by a tariff on Connecticut wood and protecting its farmers by duties on New Jersey butter, Boston was boycotting Rhode Island grain, and Philadelphia was refusing to accept New Jersey money. New York was massing troops on its Vermont frontier and Pennsylvania soldiers were committing atrocities against Connecticut settlers in the Wyoming Valley. All this was happening in the same year when, as it turned out, these same suspicious and disputing commonwealths managed, nevertheless, in the space of one hundred days, to complete the Constitution which soon joined them in federal union, abolished all trade barriers between them and is now the oldest written Constitution in the world— one which, moreover, has been copied by many new nations.

This happy example of how quickly disunity can vanish before the compelling logic of a need for action can encourage us today as we consider the situation confronting those nations which make up what has been aptly called "Atlantica." True enough, those nations—until recently moving so swiftly and hopefully toward ever larger areas of common action—are now stalled after the veto of Britain's entry into the Common Market. Indeed, there is much gloom these days about the future on both sides of the Atlantic—almost as much as Josiah Tucker, Dean of Gloucester, expressed in 1787 when he said: "As to the future grandeur of America, and its being a rising empire under one head, whether republican or monarchical, it is one of the idlest and most visionary notions that ever was conceived even by writers of romance."

We of the Atlantic Institute have been proceeding on more optimistic assumptions, based, we believe, on hardheaded and practical realism, on logic which we regard as truly compelling. Since the compelling logic of today's world—whose shrinking boundaries and interrelated problems make old nationalisms obsolete—is for coordinated action, we have not only assumed that it will come. We have made so bold as to try to chart its most desirable course, to lay down concretely, as our sub-title indicates, a plan for action. The Institute came into being on January 1, 1961, as an organization of private citizens which seeks, as an "idea laboratory," to mobilize the best brains of the free world to find solutions to our common problems. It is the only organization making such comprehensive studies under international, as distinct from national, auspices. Accordingly, its reports, of which this is the first, represent an international approach.

Soon after the Institute began its actual operations in November, 1961, the Board of Governors decided that one of the most urgent problems was the relation between America and Europe's swiftly growing, phenomenally successful Common Market. Impressively, all the eminent men invited to guide this study (their names are on page viii) accepted. Five meetings of experts were held (whose names are on pages 111-112), comprising working groups on four different subjects—economic and monetary policy, trade policy, agricultural policy and institutional arrangements—plus a "rounding-up" meeting. The members of the "Steering Committee" held three successive meetings at Institute headquarters in Paris, read the papers and made many personal contributions to the final report. What emerges is a call for an Atlantic Partnership—a partnership, moreover, of equals, based on the assumption that the United Europe now being forged in the Common Market will soon equal, if not exceed, the United States in its total wealth, manpower, resources and trade.

This emerging reality of a United Europe is the fruition of a dream, which time and again has captured Europe's most creative minds. Four times, in the two thousand years since Christ, it has begun to take form, only to be shattered. By the time Hadrian set limits to the Roman imperium, its common language and common citizenship had covered Southern and Western Europe, North Africa and the Near East. "What is more extraordinary," writes Edgar Ansel Mowrer in *Horizons,* "this empire's prestige was such that it inspired pride of belonging to it in men as diverse as St. Paul the Jew and Alaric the Visigoth. . . . Not Rome's fall itself could destroy the Western people's conception of the world they knew as a single entity."

Again, four centuries later, under the impact of Islam's invasions, Charlemagne's great new Frankish kingdom ruled from Hamburg to Rome, merging into the Holy Roman Empire—an international community of knights and theologians possessing a common religion, language, social structure and engaging —in nine crusades—in common action. "At its height, in the mid-thirteenth century," observes Mowrer, "the University of Paris attracted scholars from all of Europe, among them Albertus Magnus from Germany, Bonaventura and Aquinas from Italy, and Roger Bacon from England. Students from whatever country felt at home."

This "Third Europe" was torn to shreds in the wars of religion and dynastic succession, yet out of these failures to unite came the "Fourth Europe" of the Enlightenment, when, as Harold Nicolson observes, "culture was more international or cosmopolitan than it had ever been since the Middle Ages. Writers, artists and thinkers did not regard themselves as the natives of any particular country. They looked upon themselves as citizens of what they called the Republic of Letters." But this Fourth Europe died in a century of unbridled nationalism culminating in the First World War in which Europe all but destroyed itself. In its aftermath Winston Churchill would write in *The World Crisis* in 1930:

The curtain falls upon the long front in France and Flanders. The soothing hands of Time and Nature, the swift repair of peaceful industry, have already almost effaced the crater fields and the battle lines which in a broad belt from the Vosges to the sea lately blackened the smiling fields of France. The ruins are rebuilt, the riven trees are replaced by new plantations. Only the cemeteries, the monuments and stunted steeples, with here and there a mouldering trench or huge mine-crater lake, assail the traveler with the fact that twenty-five millions of soldiers fought here and twelve millions shed their blood or perished in the greatest of all human contentions. . . . Merciful oblivion draws its veils; the crippled limp away; the mourners fall back into the sad twilight of memory. New youth is here to claim its rights, and the perennial stream flows forward even in the battle zone, as if the tale were all a dream.

Is this the end? Is it to be merely a chapter in a cruel and senseless story? Will a new generation in their turn be immolated to square the black accounts of Teuton and Gaul? Will our children bleed and gasp again in devastated lands? Or will there spring from the very fires of conflict that reconciliation of the three giant combatants, which would unite their genius and secure to each in safety and freedom a share in rebuilding the glory of Europe?

The answer, as we now know, was both yes and no. There was yet to be another chapter, another generation immolated, in the cruel and senseless story. Even as Churchill wrote, Adolf Hitler was sweeping toward that triumph of bestial fury, of ignorance and hatred enthroned, which brought on history's most unnecessary war. But also, as Churchill wrote, the forces of European union were taking inchoate shape. The idea was old; William Penn had urged it, in England, in 1693; Washington himself, in a letter to Lafayette, prophesied a "United States of Europe"; and Victor Hugo in 1859 predicted that "the United States of Europe will crown the Old World just as the United States of America crowns the New." After World War I, Austria's Count Coudenhove-Kalergi began his tireless movement for Pan-European Union, France's Aristide Briand had gone so far as to move it before the League of Nations and an "Investigation Committee" was appointed to explore it. In

1930, in a speech at Cologne, Dannie Heineman, an American who electrified many of Europe's street railways, outlined a program for a United Europe before an audience which included his lifelong friend, Mayor Konrad Adenauer, who would one day help to create that union.

But it was during and after World War II that Churchill himself would ask his question again, in such compelling fashion that at last the "three giant combatants" would indeed act to "secure to each in safety and freedom a share in rebuilding the glory of Europe." As early as 1940, at the suggestion of Jean Monnet, then in London coordinating supplies and armaments, Churchill proposed Franco-British union and joint nationality. In March, 1943, he broadcast an appeal for a postwar "Council of Europe." That same year, René Mayer (now a member of the Atlantic Institute's steering committee) suggested to General de Gaulle an economic federation of Europe, which doubtless contributed to de Gaulle's subsequent proposal of "a strategic and economic federation between France, Belgium, Luxembourg and the Netherlands, a federation to which Great Britain might adhere." The postwar constitutions of France and Italy, and later the German Federal Republic, all envisaged future limitations on national sovereignty. And on September 19, 1946, in his now famous speech at the University of Zurich, Winston Churchill proclaimed:

> If Europe is to be saved from infinite misery, and indeed from final doom, there must be an act of faith in the European family and an act of oblivion against all the crimes and follies of the past. . . .
>
> What is this sovereign remedy? It is to re-create the European family, or as much of it as we can, and to provide it with a structure under which it can dwell in peace, safety and freedom. We must build a kind of United States of Europe.

"These words fell on fertile soil," writes Richard Mayne in his recent book *The Community of Europe*. "In the same year a poll was conducted among 4,200 European parliamentarians, two-fifths of whom replied: of these, only 3% were in principle opposed to federalism, and in France, Italy, Belgium, and the

Netherlands more than half the lower-house deputies favored some form of European union." Various movements sprang into being which culminated in the Congress of Europe held in The Hague from May 7 to 10, 1948. Among the 750 European statesmen attending were Churchill, Belgium's Paul van Zeeland and Paul-Henri Spaak and France's Robert Schuman. The Congress called for political and economic union in Europe, a European Assembly and a European Court of Human Rights. Only two months before, the Brussels Treaty Organization— embryo of today's NATO—had been formed by Great Britain, France, Belgium, the Netherlands and Luxembourg for mutual defense against any armed attack, fears of which were precipitated by Russia's bold seizure of democratic Czechoslovakia. The Brussels Organization now called upon the Congress of Europe to submit detailed plans for a European Assembly. On May 5, 1949, after seven months of negotiations under the leadership of former Prime Minister Eduard Herriot, the Brussels powers and five other countries created the Statute of the Council of Europe, and three months later its Consultative Assembly held its first meeting in Strasbourg, choosing Paul-Henri Spaak as its first President. "I came to Strasbourg convinced of the necessity of a United States of Europe," said Spaak at the session's end. "I am leaving it with the certitude that union is possible."

Later events, however, were to make clear that such efforts at *political* union, however laudable the idealism impelling them, are apt to lead into dead ends (as indeed the Council of Europe soon began to do) unless preceded by *economic* foundations. The lessons were soon to emerge that it is unspectacular, day-to-day, concrete and specific achievements— be they in the dreary world of tariffs, grimy coal and steel or whatever—which by their own evolution *become* political achievements of the first order and make still bolder political experiments possible. What brought this lesson home was a new thing under the sun—the European Coal and Steel Community, which emerged from the Schuman Plan first proposed in 1950 by France's Foreign Minister Robert Schuman. It had very limited, though tremendously important, objectives: the joint operation of France's and Germany's coal and steel industries under the common High Authority, in an organization open to the participation of other European countries. "It is no longer the moment for vain words," said Schuman that fateful May 9, "but for a bold act—a constructive act." So began what Walter Lippmann termed "the most audacious and constructive initiative since the end of the war."

The European Coal and Steel Community scarcely could have come into being had it not been for important groundwork laid—again on prosaic, day-to-day economic lines—by American initiative. This grew out of the Marshall Plan, which, as outlined by General Marshall in 1947, embraced three basic ideas: (1) "a program designed to put Europe on its feet economically," (2) that the program be "designed by Europeans" and (3) also be "a joint one, agreed to by a number of, if not all, European nations." It was this last stipulation which required Europeans to replace the old, anarchic system of their international economic relations by a system of cooperation. What resulted was the Organization for European Economic Cooperation (OEEC).

From its birth on April 16, 1948, to the time of the Schuman Plan, the OEEC laid much of the groundwork for larger developments: it reduced quota restrictions on trade, coordinated national economic policies, established a European Payments Union in which many intra-European debts could be canceled out, encouraged the habit of consultation and cooperation in many economic fields. The Schuman Plan itself was a logical extension of such cooperation. The initiative behind the plan, recounts Richard Mayne, was that of Jean Monnet, then in charge of the French Reconstruction Plan ("*le Plan*"), and the vital economic sections were written by Pierre Uri, then one of Monnet's aides (and now author of the Atlantic Institute's present report).

The Coal and Steel Community's economic accomplishments

were important enough (by 1958 intra-Community trade in steel had increased 157 percent, in coal 21 percent). Even more important were the political precedents set by its new institutions—a form of "supranationality" subordinating national interests to those of the larger community. For example, the High Authority was not composed of national representatives, but of *independent* members *forbidden to solicit or take instructions from their governments*. Even its Council of Ministers, whose members did represent governments, were subject in many cases to majority voting. It is the precedents set by these institutions and the experience built by them which laid the groundwork for still larger ventures into international cooperation. "I was long ago struck," said the Community's first President, Jean Monnet, "by a reflection made by the Swiss philosopher Amiel who said, 'Each man's experience starts again from the beginning. Only institutions grow wiser; they accumulate collective experience, and owing to this experience and this wisdom, men subject to the same rules will not see their own natures changing, but their behavior gradually transformed.'"

And so it was transformed. This experience and this wisdom, by 1957, were to make possible the historic Treaty of Rome, which set forth the bolder concept of a Common Market in which all tariffs would eventually be abolished (they have already been cut more than 50 percent).

Total trade within the Common Market has since risen 73 percent—twice as fast as its trade with other countries. By 1961 the member governments were able to join in the Bonn Declaration, which resolved eventually *"to give shape to the will for political union already implicit in the Treaties establishing the European Communities."* All these changes are a long step indeed toward a true United Europe.

It is registered in homely, prosaic ways—the Germans are eating more French cheeses and drinking more French wines, almost any Paris Café serves Munich beer, Italians are eating more meat. A million and more workers have found jobs outside their own countries. Millions now spend their holidays touring in some country other than their own; some 300,000 Swedes visit Italy each year, many in their own cars. Inside the Common Market any sort of identity card serves as a passport.

"This intermingling," writes Drew Middleton in his new book *The Supreme Choice, Britain and Europe,*

has given Europeans a better idea of how they all live and has shown them how insignificant are the barriers that nationalism has raised between country and country. It has also revived and reinforced the old idea, never entirely dead, of a common stake in Europe, her treasures, natural and man-made, her past and her future. In Geneva I have been moved by good French Catholics admiring the memorial to the Reformation, not because they accepted its religious tenets but because here a great movement had been born in Europe, their Europe.

This sense of a common European identity is reflected in a letter recently received at Common Market headquarters in Brussels: "I live in West Berlin. I want to help build a United Europe. I'm 17 years old. I'm tall, blue-eyed, blond, reasonably pretty and can type. Can you give me a job? PS: I really do want to work for Europe."

So do many others. If you walk through the corridors at 23 Avenue de la Joyeuse Entrée—named after the tradition that new counts of Flanders and dukes of Brabant in medieval times made joyous entries into the chartered cities—one sees a nation of nations in the employees. There are 510 German girls, 449 Belgian, 325 French, 256 Italian, 187 Dutch, 74 Luxembourg girls working in Euratom, the Council of Ministers, the European Investment Bank and the Coal and Steel Community —a new kind of citizen, becoming known as the "Eurogirl."

New name plates on office buildings in Brussels and Paris indicate how widely this European concept is spreading. There are now about two hundred associations especially established on a community basis—quite literally comprising the butcher, the baker and the candlestick-maker. New abbreviations include Euromail (for makers of enamelware), Euromaisers (for maize producers), Coliped (for bicycle manufacturers), Gomac for opticians and even a Union of the Association of Fizzy Drinks.

This exciting story of what has been done, by way of ever larger cooperation, makes us of the Atlantic Institute feel that the prospect of what can be done, of what *must* be done, is equally exciting. The way of greater international cooperation and concerted action, of an Atlantic Partnership, is not only desirable but already a necessity. As Pope John XXIII says so eloquently in his encyclical *Pacem in Terris:*

Recent progress of science and technology has profoundly affected human beings and influenced men to work together and live as one family. There has been a great increase in the circulation of ideas, of persons and of goods from one country to another, so that relations have become closer between individuals, families and intermediate associations belonging to different political communities, and between the public authorities of those communities. At the same time the interdependence of national economies has grown deeper, one becoming progressively more closely related to the other, so that they become, as it were, integral parts of the one world economy. Likewise the social progress, order, security and peace of each country are necessarily connected with the social progress, order, security and peace of all other countries.

The Institute has addressed itself to this problem, and herewith proposes new institutions to take the first steps to meet it. We have addressed ourselves also to what Sir C. P. Snow calls "the imperative social truth of our age," that two-thirds of mankind "don't get enough to eat; and, from the time they are born, their chances of life are less than half of ours." And Snow adds: "The means exist for our seeing to it that the poor of the world don't stay poor. The scientific and technical knowledge which we now possess is enough, if we can find the human means, to solve the problem within a couple of generations."

In the April issue of the *Bulletin of the Atomic Scientists,*

Abdus Salam, chief scientific adviser to the president of Pakistan, wrote movingly of this problem:

It is no doubt true that from Moscow or New York the possibility of ultimate nuclear annihilation appears grimly near. But in Khartoum or Karachi the living death of daily hunger is nearer still. Fifty per cent of people in my country of Pakistan earn and live on eight cents a day. Seventy-five per cent live on less than fourteen cents (including the two daily meals, clothing, shelter and any education).

Closely related to this problem is another, of which Salam also speaks:

Year after year I have seen the cotton crop from my village in Pakistan fetch less and less money; year after year the imported fertilizer has cost more. My economist friends tell me the terms of trade are against us. Between 1955 and 1962 the commodity prices fell by 7%. In the same period the manufactured goods went up by 10%. Some courageous men have spoken against this. Paul Hoffman called it a "subsidy, a contribution paid by the underdeveloped countries to the industrialized world." In 1957-58 the underdeveloped world received a total of $2.4 billion in aid and lost $2 billion in import capacity (through paying more for the manufactured goods it buys and getting less for what it sells), thus washing away nearly all the sums received in aid. I am sure that even a fully armed world with the largest possible stockpiles of armaments can forego further impoverishing the poor in this way.

In this report, the Institute proposes specific and concrete ways the industrialized world can and should forego these windfalls. Herewith are some of its general proposals:

• That whatever windfall profits industrial countries receive because of sharp drops in the prices of tropical raw materials be in effect returned to developing countries.

• That developing countries be aided by all industrial countries in accordance with an agreed formula to share the burden.

• That the Common Market develop a monetary union, which will work closely with the United States.

• That there be international rules on dumping which conform to internal domestic rules against unfair competition.

• That tariff reductions be by uniform "linear" (across-the-board) percentages at stated intervals.

• That specific steps be taken to end the sterile deadlock in which the Western world's farm policies now find themselves and transform the seeming liability of "surpluses" into sinews for a hungry world.

In particular I call attention to the proposed creation of a three-cornered "Interim Committee," consisting of the United States, the Common Market and the United Kingdom (with the countries associated with it), which would function until a partnership between America and the Common Market has become possible. This "tripod" Committee would be obliged to heed the recommendations of a group of not more than five "public members" or Wise Men—men of towering eminence, whose views would be binding on the members of the Committee unless specifically repudiated by governments. This would put the burden of effort on those seeking to divide the free world instead of on those seeking to unite it, as has hitherto been the case. Such a device does not trespass on any nation's sovereignty. But it would do something which could be more far-reaching in the long run: it would exert a continuously stimulating effect on men's minds. And it is by changing men's minds that you change the world.

This feature in and of itself might well facilitate eventual British membership in the Common Market.

The report also recommends that the Committee should operate through functional groupings of the OECD in Paris to which nations would be invited to participate in accordance with whatever subject was under discussion. Thus Japan would take part on matters affecting finance and aid to developing countries. Argentina and Australia would take part on agricultural questions. This device, which again aims at concrete, practical and specific targets, could lay the foundation for a true free world organization as an outgrowth of an Atlantic Community. For the first time in human history, we would thus have the vitals of something world-wide, as distinct from the purely regional organizations, such as NATO, or a so-called universal organization, such as the United Nations, in which Communists and nonaligned are also members.

The last chapter sums up the policies which are proposed and the machinery to carry them out.

While neither the Board of Governors nor the experts who participated in the working groups are personally committed to all the opinions expressed in this report, we believe it deserves careful consideration and contains many valuable propositions.

Pierre Uri, the former *rapporteur* for the Spaak Committee, which created the European Common Market, and who is, I am happy to say, the Counselor for Studies for the Atlantic Institute, was both the study director and the *rapporteur* who wrote the text of the report in the original French. He deserves great credit for organizing the study, for originating most of the ideas and for writing a report which also synthesizes the ideas which came out of all of those meetings.

The English text, by William J. Miller, is not a literal, word-for-word translation of the French original, but seeks to convey to English-speaking readers with maximum accuracy, and in truly idiomatic English, the essence of the French original. Mr. Miller's quick comprehension of ideas, which are both intricate and novel, added to his capacity for lucid writing, were treasured and indispensable.

Marc Ullmann, Associate for Economic Studies of the Atlantic Institute, was manager of the project, directed the research and the secretariat, and contributed many ideas.

The Institute's thanks go to Time Incorporated Book Division for much help and good advice.

We hope that the variety of background and the personal distinction of all those who took part are some guarantee of the quality of the report which we present for the consideration of governments, of international organizations, both European and non-European, and of public opinion generally. We hope further that it will facilitate understanding between the nations of the free world; and that it will provide a comprehensive picture, should future negotiators wish to refer to it, which will make clear the increasing interdependence of all courses of international action and the means by which these courses of action can, if properly interrelated, achieve their desired results.

It is clear that the free world needs a greater capacity for timely and effective common action and it is also clear that there is in the free world a demand for such capacity which cannot be stopped, but only delayed, by individuals. The fact that there have been setbacks makes it all the more important not to drift.

We believe that many of the report's proposals stand a good chance of acceptance—and quick action by many governments. Or, again, they may stimulate other constructive action. In either case the Atlantic Institute would feel well repaid for its efforts.

Perhaps this program will thus help to pave the way for a free world which is not limited to reacting to Communist moves, but can take true and constructive initiatives of its own and thus win the war of wills and ideas on which all ultimately depends.

Our shrinking world cries for greater unity. It is a hungry world where children still cry for bread even though the abolition of poverty is now theoretically possible. To meet these challenges for imagination, for boldness, for creative common action is a job big enough to demand our finest exertions, tough enough to enlist the ablest heads, noble enough to unite the hands and hearts of men.

HENRY CABOT LODGE

SOME USEFUL DEFINITIONS

International Monetary Fund (IMF). Conceived at Bretton Woods, N. H., at a 1944 conference of 44 wartime "United Nations," to stimulate trade by granting credits and helping stabilize balances of payments. The *World Bank* was also conceived to stimulate necessary war construction.

General Agreement on Trade and Tariffs (GATT). Established in Geneva in 1947 for free nations to negotiate tariffs and arbitrate problems such as dumping.

Most Favored Nation. Under the GATT agreement above, any concessions agreed upon by any two signatories will be extended, under the "most favored nation" clause, to all other signatories.

Organization for European Economic Cooperation (OEEC). Set up in Paris April 16, 1948, to coordinate various plans for Marshall Plan aid, reduce trade barriers between the recipient nations, assist economic recovery; reorganized in 1960 as the OECD.

Organization for Economic Cooperation and Development (OECD). Enlarged to include the United States and Canada to extend trade cooperation over the whole Atlantic area. Japan also now seeking membership.

European Economic Community (EEC). Founded by the Rome Treaty of 1957, embarked on gradual, phased abolition of all tariffs among its members (France, Germany, Italy, Belgium, Netherlands, Luxembourg), harmonization of labor, transport, monetary and other policies. Now generally known as the *Common Market.*

European Free Trade Association (EFTA). Or the "Outer Seven," organized by Britain as a counterweight to the Common Market's "Inner Six." Britain planned to leave it for the Common Market but, with membership there presently vetoed, EFTA's future is unclear.

INTRODUCTION

We do not regard a strong and united Europe as a rival but as a partner. To aid its progress has been a basic object of our foreign policy for seventeen years. We believe that a united Europe will be capable of playing a greater role in the common defense, of responding more generously to the needs of poorer nations, of joining with the United States and others in lowering trade barriers, resolving problems of currency and commodities, and developing coordinated policies in all other economic, diplomatic and political areas. We see in such a Europe a partner with whom the United States could deal on a basis of full equality in all the great and burdensome tasks of building and defending a community of free nations.

—President Kennedy's "Declaration of Interdependence" at Philadelphia, July 4, 1962.

Atlantic partnership . . . will . . . be built upon two mighty pillars: America on the one side, and an integrated Europe on the other. Their constant exchange of ideas, their increasing cooperation, coordination of their action are the essence of the new order of things.

—President Walter Hallstein of the European Common Market, New York, April 24, 1962.

Our aim is to make a true European unity. Then and only then will Europe be great and strong enough to build a more equal and worthy partnership with America. The right relationship between friends and allies is the relationship of equal balance and cooperation in which no partner seeks to dominate the others or dictate to the others.

—Prime Minister Macmillan at Liverpool, January 2, 1963.

The alliance of free nations ... the mutual commitment of Europe and America, cannot in the long run preserve its self-confidence and firm foundations unless there exists in the Old World a bulwark of strength and prosperity of the same kind as the United States represents in the New World.

> —*President De Gaulle at the Château de Brühl, September 4, 1962.*

These statements speak for themselves.

Clearly there is no question of absorbing Europe into a larger grouping in which its own individuality and its effort to achieve unity would be lost. On the contrary, the establishment of a new relationship as equal partners in spheres where they need each other is dependent on the extent to which European unity is strengthened.

It is not enough just to enunciate such a conception. The course must be charted, the obstacles to be overcome must be identified, the tools that will have to be used must be found.

When the Atlantic Institute first decided to try to make its own contribution to such a job, the path seemed clear. The Common Market had strengthened European unity; it was making progress in dismantling the obstacles to trade among its members; and, by adopting a preliminary framework for a common agricultural policy, it was embarking on the second stage after which the establishment of a full, tariff-free Common Market could no longer be held up. The United Kingdom had decided to join the Common Market of whose beginnings it had once been skeptical. The major political importance of this decision was so great as to engender a strong desire to overcome lesser difficulties.

This prospective enlargement of the Common Market would make it the greatest trading power in the world and would give the United States the chance to take a big step toward freer trade. In fact, the Trade Expansion Act, passed by Congress, authorized negotiations covering the whole range of tariff items and, in certain circumstances, the actual abolition of duties.

Then, the negotiations between the United Kingdom and the Common Market were abruptly broken off. This dramatic event shook to its foundations the idea of Atlantic Partnership. This is not the place to recriminate about how this happened. The French Government has stated that the door remains open pending the day that no special issues are outstanding.

One of the problems confronting us is that reductions in customs duties exceeding half the existing rate are limited under the new American legislation to commodities in respect of which the United States and the Common Market, taken together, account for more than 80 percent of world exports. This clause is meaningless unless the United Kingdom is included in the Common Market, for it would include only jet aircraft and a few other items. But, more generally, an association between the United States and the Common Market which excluded the United Kingdom (and the countries in Europe and outside Europe which are linked to it in various ways) would leave out centers of interest and influence which are far too numerous to be ignored. Recent events, therefore, make two things clear: some of the commercial clauses envisaged by American legislation cannot be applied right away; and, more important, the institutional machinery embodying the relationship of the two equal partners-to-be cannot now be established.

The provisions relating to obstacles to trade are only part of the whole problem. If there is to be a better division of labor and more rapid expansion, and if setbacks are to be avoided, there must be rules of competition, and economic and monetary policies must be harmonized. Nor is that all; in the modern world it is urgent that the rate of expansion, currency stability, equilibrium in the balance of payments, consistent agricultural policies, more effective development aid, all must be viewed as interrelated tasks and tackled vigorously. Separately, neither the United States nor Europe can do this.

Moreover, these tasks are closely related to freer trade. Freer trade can exist only if there is a background of market expansion and balanced payments—and all these policies could in turn be nullified by tariff rivalry.

The United Kingdom's bid to join the Common Market brought a sharper realization of the interdependence of Europe and the rest of the world, and of the decisive importance of the problems of currency, agriculture and relations with all developing countries. These problems cannot be solved except within a framework wider even than an enlarged Common Market. United Kingdom membership in the Common Market would have amounted to a bet—and a reasonable one—on the likelihood of being able to advance to other far-reaching problems, and to find something more than merely limited and provisional solutions.

The present situation makes it all the more urgent and important to create quickly a workable Atlantic relationship. The difficulties which stand in the way of a common viewpoint between the member countries of the Common Market are great. But the problems cannot wait. Our duty to progress toward an Atlantic Partnership may also help to overcome divisions within the Common Market and vice versa. We must be ready for talks covering the whole field of potential economic partnership between Europe and America. Surely this would be one way along which the onward march could be resumed and the way cleared for full membership in the Common Market of the United Kingdom and those other European countries which are prepared to accept the provisions of the Treaty of Rome.

We face something much greater than a mere tariff negotiation to be carried out within a narrow time limit and in which each negotiator would count up his gains and his losses. In a great enterprise such as this, only the first steps can be sketched with reasonable accuracy.

We, the undersigned, are in general agreement with the broad and concerted approach of this report, without, of course, necessarily endorsing every point of it.

We recommend that this document be carefully considered by the governments and the international organizations concerned.

We hope to stimulate international discussion of the issues and to encourage the attempt to find common ground for the formulation of policy and so prepare for action together. The *rapporteur* of all these meetings, Pierre Uri, Counselor for Studies at the Institute, has prepared the final report which attempts to synthesize these ideas, including his own, into a coherent whole. The report represents a thorough analysis of the broad facts of the present economic and monetary position and puts forth suggestions which might provide a framework for the solution of our difficulties. Many are imaginative, some may seem daringly bold. But in many ways the economic problems faced by the nations in North America and Western Europe are new, and dealing with them will require both imagination and courage. We hope that this report will provide, as well as stimulate, both.

STEERING COMMITTEE
Raymond Aron
Kurt Birrenbach
Will Clayton
Enrico Cuccia
Fernand Dehousse
Lord Franks
Gabriel Hauge
René Mayer
Ernst van der Beugel
Henry Cabot Lodge, *ex officio*

The Under Secretary of Economic Affairs of the Federal Republic of Germany, Ludger Westrick, took part in the work, but because he still holds a high public office he considers himself precluded from signing the report since this could be interpreted as reflecting the official attitude of the Federal Republic of Germany.

1 EUROPEAN COMMUNITY AND ATLANTIC PARTNERSHIP

Recovery of Europe

AFTER the destruction, dislocation and grave shortages caused by the war, Europe's recovery is an extraordinary accomplishment. Europe's progress toward unity, rejecting the bloodshed, hatreds and division of a distant past, is one of the great events of history.

A decisive contribution to this great event was America's aid for economic reconstruction, just at the right moment. This, too, was an historic event, representing the New World's repudiation of the Old's once cynical formula of "Divide and rule." The New World's new formula was "Unite and heal."

So Europe has done. And such are the realities which today underlie, and justify, the idea and the hope of a partnership, on equal footing, between the United States and a Europe in the process of achieving its unity.

The last decade has seen a striking change in the position of Europe in relation to America and the world. In that decade, the transformation of the economic situation is in marked contrast to the salient features of the early 1950s. Then, the United States' economy, starting from an infinitely higher level, continued to develop faster than European production. America's balance of payments showed a large surplus, the "dollar short-

1

age" was still extreme. Europe, its recovery still in its infancy, was suffering formidable deficits. Moreover, Europe's deficits were aggravated, in comparison with prewar years, by the relatively high prices of agricultural products and raw materials (which Europe must largely import) compared to the prices of its manufactured goods, which provide the bulk of its receipts from abroad. Most of Europe was still dependent on assistance for its survival.

A decade later, the situation is almost totally reversed.* Europe's expansion, at least on the continent, has been much faster than American expansion. One after another, Europe's countries have not only wiped out their deficits but have amassed surpluses in their balance of payments, building up their reserves to very high levels. Where the price ratio between raw materials and manufactured goods worked against Europe, it works now in Europe's favor. The "dollar shortage" is no more; instead, Europe is accumulating dollar holdings, while America itself, despite an ample surplus of exports over imports, nevertheless has a deficit in its balance of payments as a whole— caused mainly by its private investments abroad, its continued foreign aid and its payments for overseas soldiers and arms to protect the free world.

Where Europe was then dependent on assistance, Europe is now *furnishing* assistance to other developing countries; France, in particular, is matching America's per capita contributions to such aid† and is doing still more in relation to its national product.

This affluence abroad and expansion at home have helped create an economic revolution, first with the European Coal and Steel Community, then with the Common Market and Euratom. This revolution was to break down, by calculated gradual steps, the obstacles to trade, and to pursue common economic policies. The Organization for European Economic Cooperation (OEEC), set up to arrange European cooperation

* See Table I, pages 114-115, for comparisons between 1950 and 1960.
† See Table VI, page 121.

in the administration of the Marshall Plan, had already managed to secure the removal of a large proportion of import quotas between Europe's own countries. However, it had left the elimination of tariffs outside its scope. The Common Market is going further and intends to eliminate all obstacles to trade, be they quotas or tariffs. Its creation proved to be the most powerful spur to freer trade, not only in Europe itself, but throughout the whole non-Communist world, and began to have its effect on the larger tariff negotiations. Though these negotiations may have been limited in scope, they now took on a change of direction, and slowly began to dismantle the barriers by which nations had sought ever higher levels of protection against each other's goods.

Partnership versus Cooperation and Community

Twelve years have elapsed since President Schuman of France, in an historic declaration, proposed the pooling of coal and steel resources, thus founding the first European Community. Now comes President Kennedy's declaration of interdependence, which contains three essential elements. It recognizes that the United States is no longer the sole great power in the Western world in the full sense of that term. It recognizes that another power is being born—still far behind the United States in terms of volume of production, but nevertheless of comparable size. It accepts the principles of equality of responsibility and of joint authority for making decisions, accompanied by an equitable sharing of burdens. It expresses the will to ensure that the two partners, far from setting themselves in opposition to each other, will strive together to accomplish great tasks in the interests not only of themselves but of the whole world. Thus the emerging partnership between Europe and America is different from that kind of cooperation which can group together any number of countries of the most diverse size. It must be based on concerted action by two large units—two equal partners—which of course will have to work with a host of other countries or other groups of countries.

By the same token, the concept of partnership between equals differs from the looser notion of an Atlantic Community. The intentions and objectives may be the same: both recognize common values, the will to establish closer relationships and to bring about greater unity. The difference lies in the appraisal of present realities and hence in the type of organization which under existing circumstances, might best serve the purpose.

A proposal has been put forward by an international group of influential citizens to establish immediately, as among the Atlantic countries, a High Council, an Assembly and a Court of Justice. Under the terms of this proposal, some kind of majority voting would be used in the Council. It may be doubted whether American public opinion or Congress would abide by decisions of the Council on vitally important matters which might be made in disagreement with the American Government.

It is noteworthy that the system already established in the European communities does not envisage such a situation. Indeed, in Europe a majority vote among governments is not considered a valid solution. In most cases, the concurrence of an independent body representing not each government, but the interests and viewpoint of the community as a whole, is required in order to ensure an objective decision.

The proposed organization would suffer from yet another defect: it would ignore the growing reality of the European Community and go back to the old structure in which each country was present as such, whether large or small. Thus it would split what it is now trying to unite.

By contrast, an Atlantic Partnership would start with the recognition that Europe as such has begun to exist. It would acknowledge the growing reality of this Europe already on its way toward unity. It would call for a reinforcement of this European unity so as to establish between two groupings of comparable weight the basis of coordinated action.

Such a partnership, while depending on the existence and

development of a European Community, will also recognize that the word "Community" has a special, almost technical, meaning in Europe which makes it peculiar to itself and not capable of extension to other large groupings.

The "Community" seeks solutions not only to common problems, but even to the difficulties that a *single* member may encounter.

Thus, for example, where freer trade may disrupt employment for a given member, the whole Community chips in for re-employment programs on a fifty-fifty basis—half from the Community and half from the affected nation. Another feature is the creation of a single bank to help depressed areas. Then, if one member encounters balance-of-payments difficulties, the others are to provide special facilities to tide it over the trouble. Such machinery prevents the use of emergency tariff hikes as "escape clauses," and even if a member resorted to them, it could not maintain them without the approval of the Community. Thus this Community already accepts the limitation of the sovereignty of its individual states, who regain their surrendered sovereignty by its joint exercise.

Economic Basis for the Partnership

In this way a coherent economic system comes into being. The gradual abolition of obstacles to free movement from country to country affects not only industrial but agricultural products. It affects not only products but services. It affects not merely production but the *factors* of production, be they capital or labor. The rules of fair competition affect not only the actions of states but the actions of individual enterprises. The transport policy ensures that freight rates will not be set anywhere to discriminate against anyone. The Community ensures that the freeing of trade is not blocked by cartels which would divide markets or fix prices.

The Community works toward comparable legislation in each nation, both in labor rules and in systems of taxation, to avoid

distortions that would work against a proper allocation of resources, and to facilitate the movements of men as well as goods.
And a logical outcome of the system is a common external
tariff, not only to ensure that industries competing directly
with each other enjoy the same prices for imported supplies,
but also to mark the frontier between those who submit to the
same set of rules and the producers who remain outside of
this area of common economic policy.

All this makes the Community an integral entity peculiar to
itself.

America's rules and procedures present fundamental differences.

America's President does not have the power, common
to European chiefs of government, to negotiate freely on tariffs.
The American Executive must obtain prior authority to negotiate, and the limits of that authority are laid down by law
in advance. Consequently, just as the Atlantic Partnership is,
to begin with, only an idea which has to be given an exact
meaning, so the Trade Expansion Act furnishes only a framework and provides certain limits. It will be for the negotiators
on both sides to exploit to the fullest the opportunities it offers.

Those new opportunities derive from two basic features of
the Trade Expansion Act. One authorizes *across-the-board* reductions of duties in contrast with the old *product-by-product*
negotiation. The second is the extension of help through public
funds to enable those who have been injured by tariff reductions to make necessary adjustments. Such aid would be extended to *individual cases* in contrast with procedures which
would apply protective measures to *entire industries*.

In adopting these provisions America has thus borrowed from
the European model.

There are nevertheless major differences between the obligations imposed by the Common Market on the nations of Europe
and the opportunities which the Trade Expansion Act provides
for transatlantic economic relationship.

• The Common Market makes no exceptions to the principle

of free trade. American legislation, on the other hand, excludes some products from tariff cuts.

• The Community must approve any re-establishment of a protective measure, which may be used only as a last resort and only temporarily. American legislation provides for the maintenance or re-establishment of duties as a safety measure. Such unilateral action should be in fact limited by the provisions for adjustment. Nevertheless it contrasts with the Common Market's obligation to bow down to a community rule.

• The Common Market prescribes the total abolition of all obstacles to trade. America's Trade Expansion Act stipulates a general rule that duties may at most be reduced by half of their original value. This limit can only be exceeded on the following: products on which the initial duty is below 5 percent, agricultural products where American exports may be encouraged, tropical products where the Common Market liberalizes its import terms equally, and those products of which the U.S. and the Common Market together export 80 percent of the world market.*

• The Common Market is a customs union, whose common external tariff governs its relations with the outside world. America's tariff reductions, under the new law, apply to all countries enjoying "most-favored-nation" status, except Communist countries—although they may be suspended for countries deemed to have unjustified restrictions on U.S. exports, particularly farm products.

All these differences merely serve to emphasize the impracticality of expanding the Common Market into an Atlantic grouping, as compared with the growing necessity of practical negotiations between the United States and Europe. And the closer relations which the United States and Europe must establish with each other cannot exclude the equally close relations which the United States maintains with the other Americas and with certain parts of Asia; that Europe must maintain with Africa, and Great Britain with the Common-

* See Table III, page 117.

wealth. On the contrary, all this emphasizes still more that the negotiations between the two greatest partners must be conducted in the context of a *world* policy.

The heart of the matter is that the negotiations are imperative, not only because they are a good political *idea*, but because they are an economic *necessity*.

If, for example, Europe's external tariff were to have the effect of making American exports to Europe more difficult, America's "gold drain" would get worse, and the only way the United States could restore its balance of payments would be by means which Europe would have good reason to fear.

These means are obvious. Since the drain is due, not to a deficit of American exports, but largely to foreign aid and supporting troops abroad, America's quickest recourse would be to cut its aid to developing countries, and reduce the military protection it now provides for itself and its allies—or else undermine the dollar's own stability by devaluing the currency. Bear in mind that a large proportion of Europe's reserves are held in United States currency, and, however strong Europe's economy has become, it is still sensitive to the ups and downs of the American economy. So, just as America is under the economic necessity to restore its balance of payments, Europe has an equal necessity to help it do so, and thus avoid those extreme measures which would be upsetting and dangerous to both.

Europe must still consider other economic necessities as regards the shaping of its own external tariffs and export policies. The Common Market is today the foremost commercial power in the world, by virtue of the volume of its trade and of the markets it provides for the rest of the world, both in raw materials and manufactured goods.

Even without its internal trade, an enlarged Common Market —including the United Kingdom—would account for about one-third of world trade. Obviously, then, the more liberal its policy on admitting goods, the more goods it can expect to sell to others.

The practicality of such a liberal policy is easily demonstrated. Europe's industries which are best able to export will obviously be the most productive and the most enterprising, thus making the greatest contribution to Europe's internal expansion. It is therefore in the obvious interest of the Community as a whole to develop these industries to the utmost, by allowing them access to markets commensurate with Europe's own place in the world. The necessary negotiations involve not only the United States, but the world.

America's Trade Expansion Act, except for authorizing adjustment aid, deals only with trade negotiations. However, its very preamble makes clear that it does not intend to exclude a comprehensive examination of all the conditions and policies making for freer trade.

Though its primary objective is to encourage the development of U.S. exports, the Act and the President's message proposing it also express the desirability of giving the consumer the most efficiently produced goods available. They cite the expansion of the economy as one essential aim. Another is the establishment of close relations with the European Community —relations of an economic, but also explicitly political, kind. They espouse the help which the most advanced countries can give the developing countries by liberalizing their trade, but by no means rule out the maintenance of aid proper, which must go hand in hand with the opening up of enlarged markets.

Thus it is already recognized that all moves toward freer trade inevitably raise still larger problems of action.

As soon as agricultural products are involved—as they immediately are in trade negotiations—the domestic agricultural *policies* of the two partners must necessarily be considered. Nor is this enough. The world-wide implications must also be dealt with.

Mutual development policies must also be rethought, having in mind that the "most-favored-nation" clause applies to the less developed as well as to the industrialized countries.

Furthermore, policies of full employment and industrial

growth also become involved, since experience makes it abundantly clear that freedom of trade cannot be long maintained unless expanding economies ensure full employment and economic growth—and unless, moreover, acceptance of competition is not called in question by balance-of-payments crises.

In sum, then, the development and success of the Common Market *now make the Atlantic Partnership both possible and necessary*. It must deal not only with freer trade but with all the essential aspects of economic policy.

The framing of a common policy not only is a *condition* of freer trade, but in the present world situation is the main *objective*.

Indeed, the tasks which henceforth must be tackled jointly are of such a magnitude and urgency that, in a large sense, the lowering of trade barriers is the necessary *prelude* to concerted action.

Neither the United States nor the European Community, acting alone, can manage such enormous tasks as these:

• To ensure that European expansion maintains its healthy pace of recent years.

• To regain for the United States the conditions for an American rate of expansion comparable to that of Europe.

• To put the monetary system of the West on a basis which reconciles the conditions needed for expansion and for stability.

• To open new vistas for agricultural policies which have everywhere reached deadlock.

• To coordinate all actions toward the developing countries along lines which will ensure that they are in fact effective.

Lowering of Tariffs and Common Policies

All these problems cannot be solved by either Europe or the United States acting alone. Even solving them jointly cannot be prescribed by hard-and-fast formulas, tied down to some prearranged timetable.

We hear talk of a so-called "Kennedy round" of tariff negotiations. It is neither expedient nor right to think in such terms. We face not a round, but a continuing process—a joint venture which we should embark on together and learn to live with, year in and year out.

There is no deadline, no question of winner or loser; these are common problems which we must solve together.

The proper purpose of a plan of action is to identify the problems, distinguish the genuine difficulties from imaginary obstacles, lay down the principles underlying the action and chart the courses it may take.

Above all, it should provide for the instruments of discussion and decision which, when circumstances permit, will enable the principles to become action.

Procedures alone are not enough, without guidelines for them to follow.

Rules alone are not enough, without means for carrying them out.

A combination of principles, guidelines and procedures, accompanied by a coherent program of action, were the very essence of the Rome Treaty of 1957 whence sprang the flourishing Common Market of today. Today's task is more complex, the new grouping required must be more flexible, but the following chapters will attempt to sketch the main lines of the interdependent action which the occasion demands.

The occasion must be met, for in years to come the policies adopted by the partnership may well decide the history of the world.

2 COMMERCIAL POLICY

THE GOAL: *To remove the obstacles to freer trade between America and Europe, and to make possible joint commercial policies, particularly with regard to developing countries.*

W̲HAT are the chief difficulties that will beset the notion of freer trade* between Europe and America, at least at the beginning? Many of these difficulties are misconceptions, based on mistaken notions.

Businessmen on both sides are quick to believe that their competitors in other countries have unfair advantages over them.

For their part, Europeans are frightened by the high productivity of America, which comes from its formidable equipment, huge internal market and large, continuous production runs.

The Americans, for their own part, are frightened by Europe's lower wages, fearing that they could be undersold in free competition.

Neither fear is valid, when taken by itself.

It is neither productivity nor wage levels which determine competitiveness; it is the relationship between the two.

For example, if higher labor productivity is accompanied

---

* See in Table II, page 116, a summary of the trade of the partners between themselves and the rest of the world.

by higher wages, the cost of goods will not fall. Or, if wages are low but productivity is also poor, the unit cost of the same product will not necessarily be cheaper. This fact must be accepted by Americans in their relations with the Europeans, who must themselves accept it in their relations with other countries where wage levels are considerably lower—Japan, India, Latin America, for example.

Moreover, labor costs are not made up of wages alone. In the Common Market countries labor costs also include extremely high payments, in proportion to wages, for fringe benefits—paid holidays, old-age pension funds, sickness benefits and contributions to family allowances. Such contributions may add 50 percent or even more to the wage cost and can, in some cases, actually double the income of the worker. And, of course, labor is only one factor in the unit cost of product, others being the cost of materials, power, transport and the price of external services used in production.

If a market becomes united, prices will become comparable. Yet this does not require wages to be the same. Even if they were, the combination of circumstances which would cause equal wages in different countries to lead to equal prices is extremely unlikely. That would require labor productivity and other cost factors to be identical, or else the difference in costs would have to offset, exactly, the difference in labor productivity. Actually, this could happen with firms equally well placed in the Common Market, since all the same resources are available to all the firms, and the external tariff places them in a comparable position on outside materials; moreover, the increasing mobility of labor is tending to equalize wages. But the point is that this kind of uniformity, far from being indispensable, *could even tend to restrict rather than stimulate trade.*

Actually, trade is all the more profitable when there are differences in the structure of costs, with uneven effects on various kinds of production. An obvious example is the relationship between countries where labor is cheap and capital expensive, and those where capital is plentiful and wages are high. Common sense would call for cheap-labor countries to concentrate on production calling for a large labor force doing less mechanized work and for high-wage countries to concentrate on costly tooling and highly skilled labor.

This simplified example leads to an important point:

There is a strong tendency to confuse competitive conditions in a particular industry with those in economies as a whole.

A country's over-all production simply cannot get, and keep, an over-all advantage over that of other countries.

If it did, it would not only gain an export surplus of goods and services, but the surplus would quickly become so cumulative that the country concerned, in order to keep its customers from running out of money to buy its goods, would have to give them credit at a rate which would soon become impossible to maintain. Or else it would have to revalue its currency to make imports cheaper and exports more expensive. And if it did not, the inflationary effects of export surpluses would soon raise its costs enough to restore the balance.

Another mistaken notion is that the cost relationships existing in a closed market would remain the same under conditions of freer trade. One country's national market may be so narrow as to make it impossible to profit from the economies of large-scale production. Wages cannot be improved very much in countries which depend on exports to pay for their essential materials, when their trade outlets are restricted by high tariffs elsewhere. Neither condition would remain the same under free trade.

The fundamental effect of competition is this:

It stimulates all concerns to modernize their plants, to streamline their methods, to rationalize their production.

As a result, a given industry will enlarge its markets, thus gaining a comparative advantage as its costs diminish. But this happy situation will not last forever. Soon, some costs will begin to rise again and before long will gain the ascendant over costs that are diminishing.

The reasons for this are simple enough: Technical economies are not unlimited. Moreover, there is a scale of production beyond which gains become negligible or nonexistent. At the same time, labor claims its share in the benefits of rising production, and the need for increasing materials, from wider sources, means that expanding industries obtain these materials under conditions that are increasingly costly.

All these facts form the basic economic justification for using gradual mechanisms in lowering trade barriers. It is not simply to avoid abrupt changes, thus giving concerns sufficient time to adapt themselves to the new situation. A more important reason is this: *Once trade has begun to expand and competition to be felt, the relationship between production costs is no longer what it was at the outset.*

Thus, the adjustments called for by abrupt liberalization would be far in excess of what would be induced by a gradually established freer trade.

The economy as a whole must benefit, not lose, when the shifting of its resources makes for more productive use, and thus, in the end, contributes to a faster rate of expansion and a higher standard of living. This involves problems which cannot be solved by tariff negotiations alone. But these negotiations are a prerequisite for the pursuit of common policies. If the reciprocal reductions of tariffs are not to be blocked at an early stage, the establishment of some simple rules is indispensable.

Pinpointing the Obstacles

What, precisely, are the chief obstacles to reciprocal tariff reductions between America and Europe?

Most of them became clearly evident in the 1961 tariff negotiations which the United States initiated with the Common Market within the framework of the General Agreement on Trade and Tariffs (GATT). Europe has offered an across-the-board reduction of 20 percent in its common external tariff as against American concessions on specific items which were of interest to European exporters. But the United States was tied by the old reciprocal trade law and therefore offered a new list of products of lesser appeal to the Europeans. Quite often, those items on which the U. S. proposed reductions—such as automobiles—were those in which the existing tariff was already quite low. In the case of autos, it was only 6 percent. Obviously a 20 percent reduction in a tariff which is already as low as 6 percent doesn't amount to very much (actually only about $21.50 per European car). On items where tariffs were high, but not prohibitive, and where a 20 percent reduction would be significant, the United States felt itself precluded from negotiating.

This explains why actual cuts were, on the average, only about 6 percent as against the 20 percent which should have been negotiated.

This leads to the conclusion that, since the European Community can negotiate across-the-board reductions, the United States must have similar flexibility and broad powers to negotiate with it as an equal partner. The new Trade Expansion Act provides these powers in part, but many limitations remain.

Another lesson to be drawn from the 1961 negotiations is that high-tariff items inevitably lead to special difficulties.

If, for example, a European tariff were already at 10 percent, and America's at 75 percent, the negotiation of a 20 percent cut in each would be far from having the same effect: a tariff already sufficiently low would be reduced to 8 percent, but one prohibitively high would still remain prohibitive at 60 percent. In fact, Europe has only seven types of non-agricultural products on which the common external tariff exceeds 25 percent, and the maximum (applied only to carpets) is 40 percent. The United States has 110 types of nonagricultural products for which protection is easily 50 percent, in many cases even 75 percent.* Generally speaking, these are products which, even if the United Kingdom joined the Community, would not be in that category, under the Trade Ex-

* See Table VII, pages 122-123.

pansion Act, which could be reduced to zero; a 50 percent reduction would be the limit. True, a very high tariff may not be prohibitive if the costs of the protected industry are extravagantly high. Yet, obviously, even a 50 percent reduction on *prohibitive* tariffs may leave them still at a prohibitive level. The nominal value of the concession may seem impressive, but in economic terms have no real effect.

But the question of high tariffs is only a special manifestation of a more general problem, which is the average level of protection. The standard way of assessing the protective effect of tariffs is to measure the total value of tariffs levied against the total value of imports. No procedure could be more misleading. In an extreme example, a country which levied *no* tariffs on goods which it did not produce itself, but *prohibitive* tariffs on all items which it did produce, thus excluding imports, would look quite "liberal" by such arithmetic.

The real protective effect of tariffs should be measured, not against *actual* imports, but against *potential* imports. The most valid gauge of that is the internal demand—i.e., the size of the market itself.

One principle must be kept clearly in mind: *the more a country's tariff rates vary, as between different items, the wider the spread in a country's tariff system, the more protective its system is.* Europe's external tariff has relatively little variation between different products; America's has a very wide range.

The European Community's tariff has relatively little variation for the reason that it is calculated, in principle, like the arithmetical average of the four pre-Community tariffs in the Common Market area. So calculated, it tends to level out differences.

And an absolutely flat rate of duty would be equivalent, actually, to an exchange rate for importing which would be less favorable than the exchange rate for exporting. Such duties, when levied on raw materials or semifinished goods, reduce the effective protection for finished goods, which then have to compensate for the increase the tariff makes in their raw-material cost components. Ultimately, it is the *difference* between duties on a given product and on its components which reveals the amount of tariff protection in a given industry. Put more simply, it is the difference between the *average* level of duties and the tariff applicable to a *given* item which reveals it. In the hundred-odd American cases cited, compared to the increasingly uniform level of Europe's tariffs, the difference is very great.

The normal level of tariffs, however, is not the only thing that counts; one must also know the basis on which they are calculated. Broadly speaking, European tariffs are calculated on the basis of the price of the goods at the customs office, including the costs of shipping and insurance. American tariffs are calculated on the basis of the price at the factory doorstep, which is a sizably lower base. To be sure, the situation is actually not that clear-cut. American rules of evaluation give great discretion to the customs officials, so that there is very real uncertainty as to the duties to be paid. In particular, there are strong objections in Europe to the practice of "American selling price." This practice substitutes for the invoice the price of an equivalent article produced in the U.S. and applies the rate of duty on that basis. This obviously greatly raises the effective level. Fortunately, this system has been limited to very few items.

Moreover, the classifications used as regards the common European external tariff and the U. S. tariff are not the same. In some cases, where comparisons would be useful, they are difficult, if not impossible, to make. One serious problem arises from the fact that American classifications are extremely detailed and apply especially high protection to some specific and unusual items. In this way a very high degree of differentiation is achieved. Besides, such a detailed breakdown has another consequence: for lack of broad categories, some products are not mentioned by name, the duty being assessed by analogy with other products, choosing the one which is subject to the highest rate. Conversely, some products consisting of several different components, like ferrous alloys, are not singled out, but are dutiable on the basis of the most expensive component.

All these basic facts must be known and understood by both sides. The rules of evaluation would have to be streamlined. But the problem of fluctuation remains a major difficulty. Fortunately, the President, under the new Act, has considerable latitude in assessing the *relative* value of concessions obtained, in exchange for concessions granted. A realistic assessment of reciprocity might well conclude that it would be compatible for the reduction in the common tariff to be lower than the *average* reduction of the U.S. tariff.

A mutual understanding of these general characteristics of tariffs would allow simple techniques to be applied for cutting them. In any event, the idea of negotiating such cuts product by product, case by case, must be abandoned. The greatest single contribution of the Trade Expansion Act is to make this possible. It is also necessary to abandon the idea that the equivalence of mutual tariff concessions can be measured by "weighting" these reductions in relation to the value of exports. As we have seen, this is a false measurement, has no valid meaning; efforts to use it have led to fruitless discussions in the past, and its complexity alone is sufficient grounds to drop it.

The method of tariff reduction provided by the Rome Treaty is enlightening. Some of the governments were afraid to commit themselves to straight, across-the-board reductions. They were reassured by a flexible method, which required only a minimum of 5 percent reduction on each product at each stage of the tariff reduction process, with an *average* rate of reduction, in over-all tariffs, of 10 percent each time. In practice, such a flexibility was not used. Linear (across-the-board) cuts were made and at an even faster rate than scheduled: in two years, cuts of 20 percent each were made, and in the four years since 1959 have already passed 50 percent. But if the more flexible method had been applied, there would have been a difference of rhythm in specific cuts, additional time for certain products that require it would have been allowed, and this concession would have been offset by speeding up the reductions on other products. This use of an average which gives varying "weights" to different products has no fundamental drawback, so long as the end goal for every product—without exception—is the total abolition of tariffs. But if, as is still true in the Trade Expansion Act for most products, there is an absolute limitation on the reductions applicable to each product, there is no way of using such a "weighted average" without, ultimately, shrinking the general rate of tariff reductions.

The Road Ahead

All this leads to one conclusion:

The only simple and effective method which can be advocated for the forthcoming negotiations is a uniform rate of reduction on all products. But the rate of reduction granted by the various parties could differ.

Some flexibility undoubtedly will be necessary, which would be provided by giving each party the right to exempt certain products from the uniform rate. However, if the method itself is to work, such exemptions must be a limited fraction—the easiest formula being a specific percentage of a given country's imports. We have already seen why this is not the perfect solution: where tariffs are so high as virtually to choke off any imports, import figures provide no true measure of their effect. *Thus this would work only if the potential trade is appraised for items whose tariffs are now prohibitive.*

Ideally, all such exceptions sought by each country should be economically rational—i.e., products which would suffer a disadvantage from competition, either because of protection afforded the raw materials that go into them, the sale of these materials (as in the case of U.S. cotton) at lower prices to competitors, or different wage structures affecting an industry in a special way. Obviously, however, some requests will be based on political necessities. Discreet preliminary talks should make it possible to establish reasonable bounds to these exceptions. The aim should be to avoid giving a permanent character to them; rather simply to allow more time, as the Rome Treaty did, for these products to move in turn toward the abolition of tariffs. It is on record that the American tariffs on some 412 products have not been reduced for more than thirty years. It would therefore be a decisive step to unfreeze some of these products in the forthcoming negotiation.

All this will make it possible to make a start, at least, on across-the-board slashes. At present, the U.S. law does not allow drastic reduction of the highest duties. If, however, a point is reached where they cease to be prohibitive, their further reduction opens a wide opportunity for trade. The across-the-board method does make the reductions proportionate to the initial level of the duties; the higher the duty, the bigger the cut will be in actual value, thereby reducing its protective nature.

Moreover, the Trade Expansion Act provides a minimum period of five years for the reductions to take effect. In most cases the total possible reduction is 50 percent. Assuming that a yearly reduction of 10 percent is adopted, it would take five years to exhaust the 50 percent permissible. By that time, hopefully, the conditions will have been fulfilled for British entry into the Common Market, and the law's more liberal provisions can then apply—i.e., for total abolition on those many products in which the United States and the expanded Common Market would make up 80 percent of the world's trade. Accordingly, there is no practical advantage in seeking an immediate amendment to the Trade Expansion Act to make this 80 percent clause more flexible; therefore the political risk of reopening the Act is best avoided.

The Problem of the "Most-Favored-Nation" Clause

As soon as the United States and Europe, the two major industrialized groupings, start to remove the obstacles to freer trade, a new problem immediately arises: their mutual relations with the rest of the world.

Consider why this is so:

Any customs reductions agreed on, between the two major partners, will be designed to be extended to all countries benefiting from the "most-favored-nation" clause.

Actually, as often confirmed in practice, the most-favored-nation clause frequently tends to restrict, rather than enlarge, liberalism in trade. It does this by limiting the reduction of tariffs to the level which will keep out some of the best-placed challengers. To take just one example, the United States keeps a very high duty on thermometers—against its chief rival, Hong Kong, but also including Europe. It does this, not because it is afraid of European competition at all, but because it *is* afraid of the low-wage, low-cost competition of Hong Kong. So Europe also must pay the high duty.

If freer trade were to be limited simply to the two partners, the exemptions each would ask—unless they reflected imaginary fears—should be made up of different items: those in which each partner is justified in fearing the competition of the other.

Because of such outside competition, the United States and Europe, instead of having dissimilar lists of exemptions, may possibly find themselves drawing up a common list. In any case, their own negotiations will lead immediately to such broader, multilateral negotiations as can only take place within the framework of GATT. In assessing the reciprocal reductions to be asked of such third parties, in exchange for the concessions agreed by the two major partners, no automatic criterion can be used to measure the anticipated advantages. Here, as before, the measurement must be the degree of protection afforded by the tariffs, i.e., not only the average level but the extent of variation between different items.

In the case of industrialized countries, the partners will insist on equivalent advantages. But the underdeveloped countries will require different treatment, different thinking. The need for a coherent commercial policy toward these developing countries quickly becomes imperative. Many argue that simply opening trade outlets for these countries could make developmental aid unnecessary. This is true only to the extent that trade barriers imposed by the developed nations prevent the developing ones from balancing their payments, or foreign trade income-and-outgo. In this case, aid acts as a compensation.

However, there is a basic difference between the effects of aid and of increased export possibilities. Exports represent a drain on the resources of the exporting country, whereas aid represents a net *addition* to these resources. In other words, foreign aid takes the place of the savings which are so very hard to take from low incomes, and it can develop projects without curtailing the little consumption that already exists.

But all the same, it would make no sense at all to help these countries develop, to try to create jobs for their people, and at the same time refuse to provide them markets for this new-found production. The alternatives are quite clear: Aid, if followed up by the opening of markets, will tend, of its own momentum, to eliminate itself. If not so followed up, our countries will either condemn developing countries to perpetual poverty or condemn themselves to perpetual aid. Public opinion must be made increasingly conscious of the inexorable necessity of these choices.

Yet the necessary policy cannot be evolved overnight. What complicates the problem is that some countries, already semi-industrialized, may have islands of modern industrial production—employing the latest techniques, and giving proof of high productivity—in an economy where the general level of productivity and income is still low. Moreover, these countries —Japan was an outstanding example—usually suffer from overpopulation on the farms, a pressure which also keeps wage levels low. In such cases, the outstanding industries can combine high productivity with low wages and their costs are much below those of more advanced countries.

The instinctive defense of industries threatened by such competition is to build permanent protective barriers. This is not necessarily the best thing for the whole economy. In an advanced economy, there may well be other activities in which the affected industry's resources could produce higher yields —for example, a typewriter producer might switch to computers. Frequently the maintenance of threatened industries is a burden to the whole community. Nevertheless, their sudden closing would throw men out of work, and waste the resources left suddenly unused. The answer, then, is a concerted policy which is both gradual and whose effects are spread over a wide area.

It was brave and generous of the United Kingdom to decide to open its textile markets to Indian and Hong Kong producers. But the result of this isolated gesture—a virtual prostration of Lancashire's own textile industry—in the end provided a justification for other countries to practice protectionism. Had the impact of this competition been spread over wider markets, and over a longer period, the result could have been beneficial to all. It is imperative, therefore, for the industrialized countries to decide on a common attitude and a concerted policy.

Once again the key to the solution is time. It offers gradualness, and the sort of transition period which, as in the Common Market, gives concerns a breathing spell during which they can adapt themselves to the realities of competition. Its practicality is based on the fact that, as freer trade develops, cost factors do not remain stationary on either side. The most illuminating example is Japan itself, where a progressive increase in wages is keeping pace with the development of production and exports. As for the countries which must accept increased imports, a progressive shifting toward new activities which can smoothly absorb the manpower and offer more productive work will provide expansion and a higher income for the whole economy.

Some argue that the advanced countries should simply open their frontiers without tariffs to the products of the developing countries. It is unlikely that such a suggestion would be "practical politics," given the immediate economic dislocation which it would cause. If the proposal is limited to raw materials, it has meaning only for the United States. Europe, which obtains almost all its raw materials through imports, already admits them virtually duty-free. If the proposal is extended to all primary products, then domestic agricultural problems immediately impose difficulties.

The differences in conditions of production will make it hard for developing countries to benefit effectively from the most-favored-nation clause. Its extension will not be refused outright, but it will tend to keep tariffs higher than the average when the developing countries are major suppliers.

What, then, is the sensible solution to this deadlock? What is needed is a policy both realistic, generous and effective:

• The industrialized countries would give up any requests for reciprocal tariff concessions from the developing countries, until such time as they had reached a certain level of real income per head.

• In exchange, they would ask these countries to help in ensuring that the *increase* of their sales of sensitive items should be *gradual*.

• In other words, voluntary restrictions on the rate of *development* of these exports would be accompanied by unilateral reduction of the customs duties payable on them.

In this way it should be possible to prevent the reduction of duties on these products from being substantially lower than the agreed average.

A proposal of this kind is an integral whole. It reconciles the conditions of growth for one party with the stability of the other, and ensures a reasonable division of labor in world production. The advanced countries must be conscious of the relocation and conversion which their economies must accept in order to absorb gradually the greater exports which the developing countries will be capable of supplying competitively. It is also the only way of giving them the money to buy the food stuffs they need and which the advanced countries urgently need to sell.

The other way leads to a shrinkage of the markets which the agriculture of the developed countries themselves should normally enjoy, thus making agriculture pay the price for industrial protectionism.

3 AGRICULTURAL POLICY

THE GOAL: *To end the sterile deadlock in which the Western world's farm policies now find themselves, and transform the seeming liability of "surpluses" into sinews for a hungry world.*

IF TODAY you look at the world as a whole, one tragic fact stands out above all others. That fact is hunger. Millions of persons are either dying or living a half-life because of inadequate diet.

For the developed countries, this statement immediately calls to mind another fact: this hunger exists despite huge agricultural surpluses. The markets and outlets for farm products are so inadequate that so-called protective measures are frequently considered necessary.

This points to another truth: that agriculture could be the rock on which all our efforts to increase world trade founder. This is a striking illustration, if ever there was one, of the indissoluble relationship between freer trade and common economic policies—in this case, the policy related to agriculture.

We, in the developed countries, thus have the opportunity together to create policies which would be less wasteful and bring a decisive contribution to the welfare of the underdeveloped countries.

In this chapter we therefore consider how we can emerge from the jungle of rigidities and protective devices in which we find ourselves, and use our financial resources to construct a great world market, overcome famine and solve our farmers' problems.

Conceivably, difficulties over agriculture could hamper tariff negotiations between America and Europe as a whole. True, on temperate products, the United States is authorized to go beyond the 50 percent limit on customs reductions—and theoretically to zero—to the extent that reciprocal concessions obtained on other markets enable the United States to increase its agricultural exports. On the other hand, the Trade Expansion Act provides for the withdrawal of industrial tariff benefits from countries which maintain, or reimpose, unjustified restrictions on American agricultural exports. However, since it is clearly in the interests of American industry to get the Common Market's external tariff lowered (America's exports to Europe being much greater than its imports from Europe), it is not likely that such a withdrawal will take place.

The real difficulty lies elsewhere. The liberalization of trade is the more easily accomplished the more rapidly expanding markets there are and provided the expansion can be kept up. During periods of recession, resistance to freer trade grows stronger. It also grows stronger in declining industries and in sectors where there is a danger of overproduction.

In the case of agriculture, there are two distinct types of products—those whose markets tend to expand rapidly with the income level of consumers and those which either remain stagnant or even decline as the standard of living rises. A simple example: people with rising incomes eat more meat but less bread. The demand for meat is dynamic, for wheat it is static or declining.

Yet the striking thing about the agricultural price policies of the developed nations, almost universally, is that *they give too little incentive to products with a rising demand, and too much incentive to those enjoying the least dynamic demand.* Such policies are bound to create obstacles to freer trade gen-

erally, and consequently trade cannot be considered inde-
pendently of agricultural policy. Yet everywhere these policies
are in a kind of deadlock.

Indeed, countries whose general policies are the most liberal
often have the most protectionist and controlled policies in
agriculture. They apply restrictions on production in agriculture
which would be inconceivable in industry. They impose restrictions on the quantity of imports—in other words, quotas—
which could never be applied to industrial products, under
GATT rules, except temporarily in cases of real trouble in
balance of payments.

To an extent, a special policy for agriculture can be justified.
Producing a pig is more difficult, in some ways, than producing
a car. The car producer can adjust his quantity to demand, and
figure his costs reasonably close. But it takes two years to grow
a pig, during which both the demand for pork and the costs of
feed can change abruptly. Production plans can be made
sensibly only if there is a measure of price stability. Such
stability is difficult in a free market, whose variations in supply,
owing to factors beyond control, such as the weather, for example, can lead to excessive fluctuations. Yet the attempt to
stabilize prices can lead, and often does, to the fixing of prices
—for political reasons—at a level high enough to stimulate
overproduction. What began as an economic *use* ends as a
political *abuse*.

The motivations of such politics are understandable. The
actual income of farmers, in a free play of supply and demand,
would be much lower than that of other workers. To remedy
this, the public authorities try to correct the imbalance through
high prices. But the higher the price, the lower the demand. In
the end, the system is more costly to the public than if direct
payments were made to supplement the income of farmers.

Theoretically, the most sensible way to raise farmers' per
capita income to the level of others' would be to reduce the
number of people working on the land. This is particularly
true in the United States, where some 12 percent of the farms

are actually turning out more than half of the total production. But it is impracticable, both politically and humanely, to do this suddenly and abruptly. Doing it gradually would be likely—at least in Europe—to increase rather than curb production because of the big increase in productivity it could create.

In any case, one basic idea must be accepted:

As long as the number of farmers is larger than production strictly requires, *systems of income subsidies to individuals are preferable to the maintenance of excessively high prices.*

They are preferable with two important qualifications:

• Such income subsidies should be geared to the direct, personal needs of those concerned, without being linked to the *volume* of production, and without incentives to increase production. A giant wheat farmer with thousands of acres of good land would neither need nor receive such assistance, which could then be devoted to the small farmer with forty acres.

• Such subsidies should also be limited in time, and applied to personal requirements, during a transitional period of relocating marginal farmers into more economically desirable activities. Such a method of adjustment is in keeping with that which the Common Market has followed, and the United States is now beginning, for *industries* affected by freer trade.

One major difficulty in the way of a rational agricultural policy is that reliable standards are not available. They are not available in regard either to the volume of production or to the price level. Let us examine these questions in detail.

Price Policies

However much the farm policies of the United States, the Common Market and the United Kingdom may differ from one another, they all have the same effect:

• They all tend to depress the level of so-called world prices.

• The more these policies contribute to lowering the level of external prices, the more their own protectionist measures have to be increased—a truly vicious circle. The only exception is in products whose trade has been limited by agreements designed to maintain prices.

Consider each system:

UNITED STATES. Support prices have been accompanied by limitations on acreage to be cultivated. Yet chemical fertilizers and other improved technology keep raising the total yield on the reduced acreage. Result: total quantities are increasing, stocks are mounting (especially wheat and corn), and the government gets rid of them abroad either at prices well below the support level or by giving them away to countries as grants of foodstuffs, i.e., aid-in-kind. It could almost be said that the level of world prices is in inverse ratio to American domestic prices—that is, the higher the latter, the lower the former.

COMMON MARKET. It has begun to provide itself with the tools for an agricultural policy, but the policy as such has not yet been fixed. The mechanism is a system of levies which makes up the difference between import prices and internal prices. These levies will gradually disappear as between the countries of the Common Market, thus bringing about a single market. But the levies on imports from countries outside the Common Market will be such as to bridge the gap between the domestic price and the lowest import price. If the size of such levies had been laid down in advance, then the price level also would have been automatically fixed—or vice versa. Only when the actual figures are determined will the *real* policy begin to take effect.

The Community's Council of Ministers was scheduled to set the internal price of wheat by April 1, 1963, but adjourned without doing so. Cereals and dairy products are the chief price-supported crops in the Community. French wheat growers produce under more favorable conditions than the German, who are high-cost growers; on the other hand, Dutch dairy farmers are far more efficient than their higher-cost French counterparts. If, for example, the price of wheat stays near its present French level of $90 a ton, little overproduction would be encouraged and most marginal production would be curtailed. If set closer to the German level of $117, not only would production by marginal German farmers be encouraged, but the French farmers would also be stimulated to overproduce tremendously. It remains to be seen what proportions of overall production will be encouraged by the prices set, and what room this will leave for imports—presently about 20 percent in the case of wheat.

In any event, the reduction of imports which might ensue from the encouragement of internal production would tend to depress world prices. Furthermore, the mechanism of the levy is based on the cheapest import price, thus forcing outside producers to align themselves when selling to the Common Market with the cheapest exporter even if he is subsidized or dumps.

UNITED KINGDOM. The British system of agricultural subsidies is just as depressing on world prices as the others. Seemingly, imports are unrestricted and duty-free, creating an appearance of a free market. Seemingly also, the consumer gets the benefit of the low prices set by such free competition. But the British farmer is paid the difference between these free prices and the support prices which he is guaranteed. *And he is paid this in proportion to the quantity he produces,* a practice which obviously tends to increase production whether it is economic or not. This additional production serves very effectively to cut down the demand for imported products.

Since the United Kingdom is the world's principal market for imported foodstuffs, any cuts in her farm production would rapidly lead—as soon as surpluses were eaten up—to a considerable rise in prices.

In sum, the subsidies are no great advantage either to British farmer or consumer, since the income of the first is no greater than that of his European opposite number, while the second must pay in taxes for the apparent savings on his food.

The subsidies keep imports cheap, and therefore also subsidize Britain's balance of payments at the expense of the major foreign suppliers of primary products. Among those primary producers are underdeveloped countries.

The Markets

The picture which emerges is the ever-increasing gap between world prices and domestic support prices. These price policies in the developed countries, for one thing, are inconsistent with each other, thus making free trade well nigh impossible; but it is also true that they encourage production even where demand is declining. What results is mounting surpluses which in turn can only be limited by direct curbs on production. The more production must be reduced by direct means, the more in turn the price is raised, in order to maintain the farmers' income. To sum up: whenever demand falls off, prices are raised again.

Under such circumstances, trade could only be maintained by requiring the importing countries to restrict their production by the same methods now being applied by the exporting ones —in short, to expect that the countries of the Common Market would follow the American practices, ineffective as they are.

But one thing is certain: the European Community will not accept, in the near future, any crop reductions by the American method of acreage control, since the development of the Common Market will itself curb production insofar as it eliminates marginal producers. As the Common Market grows, if the superior efficiency of a French wheat grower enables him to far outproduce others, surpluses are no longer to be blamed upon his production, but rather on the continuation of too much *noneconomic* growing elsewhere, which the Common Market should tend to eliminate. More and more, surplus production is coming to be regarded as due to *marginal* production.

If a deadlock is to be avoided, the attempt to develop trade in agricultural products must be pursued in the framework of an enlarged and growing market.

Only a small number of food-importing markets now pay their way—Japan, Germany and, biggest of all, the United Kingdom. These markets are "saturated," as witness the keen competition for Britain's, fought for by its own farmers, claimed by its traditional Commonwealth suppliers, coveted by the Common Market, watched jealously by the United States. Yet Britain's demand does not grow rapidly enough for it to be able to absorb the growing productivity of the Commonwealth, let alone the production of all its claimants together. *It is scarcely surprising that agriculture was the chief problem blocking Britain's entry to the Common Market.*

These saturated markets make a striking contrast to the immense needs which remain unsatisfied in the developing countries for lack of money to buy food.

At least one out of every four persons in the world—a billion people—suffer from malnutrition and go to bed hungry each night. Indeed, the United Nations' Food and Agriculture Organization claims that more than half the world's population so suffers. Its statistics may be questionable—since the minimum subsistence level cannot be defined exactly—but even if the figure were cut in half, it is still a shocking fact when science and technology have made the abolition of hunger at least a theoretical possibility.

Despite all the internal problems of "farm surpluses" among the developed nations, there is no genuine surplus for the world. On the contrary, there is a serious deficiency which is likely to grow larger. Even if one assumes that only one-fourth of the world's people is malnourished, and that their diet is no more than 20 to 25 percent inadequate, that would still mean, for the world's whole population, a present rate of food supply which is at least 5 to 7 percent inadequate.* The Western world's so-called "surpluses" represent a much smaller fraction than that of world food production.

The best land, that which can most easily be put to agricultural use at the lowest cost, lies in the industrially developed countries, including Soviet Russia. In most of the remaining areas, costly efforts and intense work are needed to develop difficult or arid land. Taking the world as a whole, the most determined effort should be concentrated not on restricting

* See Table V, page 120.

but on *expanding* agricultural production in those regions of the world where soil and climate are most favorable. If food purchasing power can be found for those countries whose un-satisfied needs are greatest, all this production and more will be needed. If the "have" and "have-not" groups do not get together, forecasts agree that, between now and the end of the century, there will be an increasing imbalance between (1) countries where the surplus of production over consumption is constantly increasing and (2) countries where population growth will inexorably aggravate the scarcity of food.

What are the proper policies to resolve this grim and tragic paradox? The fact that there is really no genuine world surplus does not mean that the major producers should not continue to reduce the population employed in agriculture. They should, since *lower productivity in this sector curbs all-round economic expansion and any possibility of increased purchasing power for the farmers themselves.* Nor does it mean that production today is on the right lines; on the contrary.

But the West must pay heed to the tragic effect on a hungry world of repeated complaints about its "surplus" production.

The United States is already giving away its surpluses to needy nations, at the rate of some $2 billion a year, either in free distribution or in allocations at a systematically reduced price. Europe will soon have to face the disposal of future surpluses in similar ways, since its farm production will in-crease, through technical progress, far more than consumption no matter how much the internal market is protected. The present $2 billion rate of surplus disposal, mostly American, compares with a need of $5 to $6 billion, even for a basic diet consisting mainly of cereals with some fat and protein supple-ments. But the real stumbling block is neither the availability of surpluses nor the desire to give them away. *It is rather the necessary unloading facilities and means of transport which would enable the neediest countries to make use of any in-creased supplies.*

An integrated system of common policies agreed upon by

the chief supplying nations would give priority to such unloading and transport facilities, which the developing nations also
need to build their own industries.

Such policies must also consider the fact that present methods
of providing food aid are often disrupting and self-defeating
and prevent the rational development of an agricultural policy.
For example:

• Distribution of surplus foodstuffs not only keeps prices
rigid but aggravates the production problem. The recipients
have no other choice than to accept what is overproduced. In
this sense distribution of surplus foodstuff helps the producers
of the surplus at least as much as it does their recipients.

• Still more serious, if countries get foodstuffs for nothing,
their markets are closed to the few developing countries which
themselves have an exportable surplus of agricultural products.
Wheat supplied to India by the United States chokes off
Burma's rice exports, as well as wheat exports by Argentina—
two countries which the United States, out of another pocket,
is seeking to help develop industrially.

• Free distribution may hold back the development of local
production.

• Such supplies, sent to countries able to process them,
can—since the actual cost of the processed products is only
partially taken into account—cause very serious distortions of
international trade, or else provoke undesirable restrictions to
offset them. Thus, for example, the distribution of surplus
American corn to Israel enabled that country to produce and
export eggs at an unbeatably low price, thus upsetting Europe's
own egg market.

A Plan for the Future

These drawbacks to present methods suggest a new one, which
could help the developing nations while opening the door to a
more rational agricultural policy and to freer trade in the
developed countries themselves. The proposal:

• Instead of food aid-in-kind the developing nations would be given monetary grants, earmarked for the *purchase* of food.

• The breaking up of bottlenecks in transport and distribution, as proposed above, would allow a gradual increase of such aid for food purchases.

• The beneficiary nation would, by gradual steps, become free to buy whatever types of food, from whatever sources, it so chose.

An essential feature of such a new policy would be an assessment of the proportion of aid available for each country which should be given in this earmarked form, and of the ways in which such aid may best be used in a given country. For some, this financing of food purchases abroad would have to be regarded as a stopgap, until domestic production could be developed by adequate technology. For them, this kind of aid would simply be a short cut, to speed up the otherwise painfully slow development of their own agriculture. Where needs are particularly grave, some free distribution of food by the government concerned may be necessary to provide subsistence for the poorest sections of the community.

Let us examine in more detail why more rational farm policies and freer trade would result:

• Demand, instead of having to be determined by production, should instead help to reorientate production to the true demand.

• Increased outlets would ensue. They are the basic condition of greater liberalization of trade, since they make further exports possible and therefore facilitate imports as well.

• A redistribution between producer countries could be organized on the basis of the commodities they can produce and ship most efficiently and cheaply.

• This redistribution would avoid the bottlenecks which otherwise the availability and cost of transport would create in the trade and distribution of food.

Joint action along these lines between the Atlantic partners, together with other large producer countries, would, taking the contributing countries as a whole, *reduce the actual cost of aid*: such aid would only have to cover the price of the commodities and transportation under the most economic conditions. Ultimately, therefore, there should be no connection between the financial contribution and the kind, or source, of goods purchased. Such a plan will immediately meet political opposition in countries where the present methods of distribution have been agreeable because they help its domestic farmers as well as the recipients. *But it is impossible to strive for freer trade and at the same time cling to a system which maintains all the rigidities of production and prices.*

Moreover, as against the fear of change, the enlargement of markets and the establishment of a more normal price level would bring an overwhelming economic advantage to the producers themselves.

As against the political objections is an overwhelming economic benefit: this bold revision of present methods would resolve, for the developed countries themselves, the problems of both price policy and market redistribution.

Such a redistribution of markets would help end the anomaly in which developed countries by-pass the vast unfilled markets to fight each other for those that are already saturated, while dumping their surpluses on each other's doorsteps.

True, it is essential for countries with a high level of agricultural productivity, like those of the Commonwealth, to have expanding, not merely steady, markets. Yet it is not necessarily essential that these markets be based on present trade routes, which in some cases even carry goods to the opposite ends of the earth. In a more rational distribution of trade, based on a broad international program of monetary aid earmarked for food, Australia might well route much of its produce to feed Southeast Asia, New Zealand provide proteins to make up nutritional deficiencies in Africa, and Burma increase its rice exports to its neighbors.

By converting the most pressing needs into effective demand, joint financial aid on the lines proposed would put an end to the present division between trading, dumping and giving. This progressive reconstitution of a true world market would gradually lead to a price level in keeping with the general equilibrium—instead of the existing gap between artificially depressed world prices and artificially increased domestic prices.

Western Europe and the United States together spend some $7 billion a year now on subsidies, price supports and surplus disposal. This $7 billion exceeds the $4 billion both are currently spending on public aid, other than food distribution, to developing nations.

Suppose they would agree to devote to such aid each year an increasing proportion of the $7 billion they are now spending on agriculture. As an enlarged market brought rising demand, prices also would undoubtedly recover, to the extent that farmers could enjoy a more normal income. They would also plan both their choice of crops and the amount of production on the market's own weathervanes, instead of the artificial and arbitrary choices dictated by price supports and production controls.

The more an enlarged demand raised world prices, the more the biggest producers would benefit, a fact which would justify their progressive raising of the total aid they give to development. Better still, higher prices brought about by an increased flow would improve the balance of payments for America and thus ameliorate a problem which tends to limit the contributions it can prudently make for development aid. Where this aid is already large, as in America, political and farming circles will want assurance that new policies will provide an equally big foreign market for farm products. In the ordinary course of things, this would happen, since increased demand will flow naturally to markets with the largest-scale availabilities. However, some provisional guarantees will be required for a limited redistribution of orders, should these depart, under the new system, too radically from the present pattern of world exports.

The decisions that face us here govern the whole future of Western agricultural production. They afford new opportunities of agreement between the Common Market and the United Kingdom, and scope for a partnership between Europe and the United States capable of dealing with all the major issues that confront the world.

The challenge is worthy of all the thought and action it requires. That challenge is to unleash the full capacity of agricultural production to the loftiest task, namely, to banish hunger from the world.

4 AID TO DEVELOPMENT

THE GOAL: *To assure continuity in aid, to share the burden equitably and to limit the adverse effect of price variations on development.*

I<small>N THE</small> case of agriculture, the Trade Expansion Act provides special treatment for products grown in tropical regions. The 50 percent limit on the reduction of tariffs does not apply. The requirement is that such products be not grown on a large scale in the United States and that the Common Market similarly reduce or abolish its own rates.

By this definition tropical products do not compete with the agriculture of developed countries. Besides, as a whole, they are grown, not to feed the inhabitants of the countries which produce them, but to be exported to the developed countries. An increase of such sales is, therefore, an essential contribution to the development of developing countries.

The prospect for such an increase of sales in the case of tropical fruits and also of fats, such as ground nuts, palm and coconut oil, is good. The markets are constantly growing. Coffee presents a very serious problem. As a result of high prices a few years ago, the number of plantations has increased, both in Latin America and in Africa. It takes a few years for a coffee tree to bear its fruit. But now production has almost doubled

41

in eight years and a glut is developing. Coffee is a product whose consumption on a world level cannot be readily increased. The United States absorbs half of the total world production, but the American market is so saturated that the level of consumption can only increase because of an increase in population, not by virtue of an increase in incomes. Asia is a market for tea, not for coffee. There are some European countries, including Germany and Italy, which levy very high domestic taxes on coffee; this creates an unfortunate impression in the developing countries, where it appears as a tax on them. But whatever increase in consumption might follow an abolition of such taxes would not significantly alter the size of the world market.

On the other hand, coffee is both easier to grow and far more profitable than other crops. The price supports which it enjoys make it difficult to determine by direct observation how a better balance could be brought about either by a reduction of the incentive to produce or by opening new outlets through cheaper prices.

A commodity agreement has now been signed which limits the exports of the different producing countries. It remains to be seen how far this will effectively curb production. It would be more equitable to demand that production be reduced most in the countries where the land can be more easily used for other crops or where incipient industrialization reduces the dependence on coffee for employment and export. Coffee is thus a clear example of overproduction which exerts a permanent downward pressure on prices.

In the case of most of the tropical products, the greatest difficulty stems from the fluctuation of prices which accompanies the fluctuation in volume of production. Furthermore, this problem extends to all sorts of raw materials and calls for comprehensive solutions which will be discussed later.

The preferences granted by the Common Market to the African countries associated with it—especially for tropical agricultural products—raise a controversial issue. The association which has been entered into by former colonies of the

Common Market countries, mostly in Africa, provides for free entry of all goods from those territories into the Common Market. Other countries do not have this privilege. This therefore creates a preference for the Common Market associates. When this applies to tropical products, Latin-American producers—and a few other African countries—protest this tariff as discriminatory and unfair.

This matter cannot, however, be judged in the abstract. It is generally acknowledged that a country may protect its own infant industries, i.e., give them a privileged market on its own territory. In the case of tropical products, the market is in the territory of the countries with which the new countries have had special relationships in the past—relationships which are now continued by a treaty of association with the Common Market. The preference which they enjoy in this market for their incipient production is not essentially different from a protection to infant industries.

However, such a solution is workable only to the extent that it favors products which are but a small fraction of world supply—like the 10 percent of world cocoa produced by Africa's French-speaking territories. Suppose that, if Britain entered the Common Market, Nigeria accepted a treaty of association; nearly 90 percent of world production of cocoa would suddenly be covered by preferential treatment. A preference covering such a large part of world production would harshly discriminate against the remaining minority. All this argues that the choice of method—as between protection, preferential treatment and subsidies—should depend on the particular situation in each country.

The Common Market system in relation to such tropical products raises still broader issues. By granting preferences, it also broadens the market for some producers at the expense of others and forces those others to reduce their price to overcome the tariff barrier. But producers not associated with the Common Market have lower costs on certain products than producers who are associated. Thus, in fact, those consequences for outside producers are mitigated to a considerable degree.

Inside the protected market some countries agree to pay to the African producers a price substantially above world prices. Such overprices are not really trade, but aid.

Some stabilization schemes are operated either by guaranteed prices or by paying into a fund a contribution to the importing country when prices are low; the resources thus accumulated are used to reduce the export price in times when it is pushed up by high demand. Thus, from the outset, the problems of trade, of aid and of price fluctuations show themselves as mutually interdependent.

No matter how liberal the import policy of the developed countries is toward the underdeveloped ones, it is likely that an increasing proportion of any expansion of world trade will come from reciprocal trade between the developed countries themselves. To a considerable extent, this trade will be in those products embodying the latest inventions and the most advanced techniques. But such an increase in trade within the developed area does not mean that the underdeveloped countries will necessarily be at a disadvantage. It is not their *relative* share of world trade that is crucial to them, so much as it is the *over-all* growth of their own export opportunities and, above all, of their resulting power to buy other countries' products. Indeed, this increase in trade among the developed countries would be very much in the interests of the underdeveloped countries themselves as it would increase the size of the United States gross external receipts and this, as we shall show, makes foreign aid less burdensome for the United States. Present United States level of development aid, at around $4 billion a year, although it is 0.72 percent of America's Gross National Product ($554 billion), does loom very large in terms of the balance of payments. What the United States pays abroad and what it receives, between $25 and $30 billion in each case, is around 5 percent of the GNP. But aid is so large a portion of the deficit, or dollar drain, that it assumes an importance out of all proportion to its relation to total domestic resources.

Sharing the Burden

Aid, to be effective, needs, above all, continuity. For the developing countries, the biggest obstacle to forming coherent development plans, and even more to putting them into effect, is the constant fluctuation of their external resources—whether from loans or grants or from the undependable value of their exports.

If aid is to be put upon a basis of continuity, with all developed nations assuming properly proportionate shares of the burden, no donor country's balance-of-payments situation should be the criterion for the normal contributions of each country—yet it may well be the actual bottleneck.

Such a coherent plan of aid should provide that any country which might have to interrupt its aid because of a payments deficit should be able to obtain short-term credits to ensure continuity. It could not, however, expect to be underwritten indefinitely while still retaining the sovereign right to decide its aid policy by itself.

Aid can be effective only if it is continuous, and it can be continuous only if it is coordinated—i.e., discussed and administered on a joint basis.

This conclusion leads to two prime needs:

• A formula whereby each of the developed nations will assume its proper share of the aid burden.

• An agreement on policies for the distribution of the joint development funds thus created.

For the purpose of devising a burden-sharing formula, only genuine aid should be included: direct grants, or loans which are of long-term and low-interest or else reimbursable in the currency of the beneficiary nation. It would not include short-term credits aimed at stimulating exports, or investments made with a view to profits. Such funds may be very helpful for the recipient country but cannot be considered as a sacrifice from the capital-exporting one.

What formula is suitable?

A country's capacity for affording aid is obviously dependent on its resources, usually measured by its Gross National Product. It is generally accepted that the point at which a country can reasonably be expected to contribute to an international aid program is when its citizens have an income per head of at least $600 a year.

Roughly speaking, the sum of the industrialized countries' GNPs is $1,000 billion. Aid of 1 percent, apart from direct investments and commercial credits, should provide $10 billion a year.

At present, this 1 percent level of aid is actually exceeded only by France. It is far from being reached by the United States, whose level is about 0.72 percent.

It would seem fair that the proportion of the national product assigned to aid should increase *progressively* with the per capita income. But aid proper will always represent a minute fraction, probably less than 1 percent, of the national product of the industrialized countries.

Thus it would be unnecessarily complicated to establish a sliding scale whereby the higher a country's real income per head, the more that country should contribute to foreign aid in relation to its GNP. But there is a simple formula which, as a practical matter, achieves the same result.

The ordinary way of comparing GNPs is to translate them into United States dollars at the current exchange rate. It must be remembered that the richer a country is, the more it spends on services like housing, doctors and education—and also the higher are the prices of such services. The higher prices of services inflate the GNP beyond a true measure of its value. Since these services do not enter into international trade, they do not affect the exchange rate. Thus the comparison of national products on the basis of the exchange rate tends to exaggerate the difference in real income per capita. For that reason the United States per capita income is three times higher in money terms than the European one, but only about *twice* as high in terms of real purchasing power.

This consideration simplifies matters considerably. A flat percentage of the national income, as recorded in current statistics, does provide virtually a scale which rises as real per capita income rises because of this tendency of the GNP itself to be inflated beyond the *true* rise in purchasing power.

An agreement on so simple a formula—an identical fraction of the national product—would have the advantage of enabling each country to know what the other is doing. In each donor country, resistance to aid is based, at present, on an *over*estimation of what it itself is doing and an *under*estimation of what others are doing.

A single formula does not mean that all contributions should be paid into a single fund. The existing links between groups of countries which are tied by tradition, mutual knowledge and experience should go on, indeed make aid more effective. Where coordination is indispensable is in regard to the amounts made available, and their distribution.

The Offset of Price Fluctuations

Such a formula, however, does not meet one of the chief obstacles to development—the fluctuation in prices of produce and raw materials which, the underdeveloped nations complain, has cost them more, over the past few years, than all the funds they have obtained by way of aid. This cost has been in the falling prices of their own raw materials compared with the rising prices of the finished goods they must buy— the "terms of trade."

Needless to say, they base this complaint on a period when prices were especially favorable to them—that of the early fifties, when a sharp rise in primary prices over prewar levels was suddenly aggravated by the sharper rises during the Korean War. To find a less distorted relationship of primary and finished prices, an average could be taken of the fluctuations in the terms of trade over a period of almost a century, and over the much shorter period of 1950 to 1962; what emerges is an average relationship not much different from that of the *actual* relationship in 1957-58.

Even on this more objective basis, and even with current price relationships more favorable for developing countries than in the past, prices have continued to move to their disadvantage, and to the advantage of the industrialized countries.

This is the problem which commodity agreements try, like that in coffee, to solve. They aim to limit the price fluctuations which result partly from variations in demand, as for raw materials, but far more from the variations of production, as in the case of agricultural products. Such agreements are in force not only for such tropical products as coffee and sugar, but also for foodstuffs from temperate zones such as wheat. Whatever the difference in other respects, all of them are based on export quotas. The extension of such commodity agreements to a broader list of commodities is contemplated, without defining precisely what the content would be.

This is not a matter on which dogmatic judgments should be passed. The attitude of the United States Government, once hostile or mistrustful, has changed notably to active support. However, an attempt is made in official statements to distinguish between short-term fluctuations—which should be flattened out—and longer downward trends which normally accompany increased productivity or simply indicate persistent overproduction. Determining which is which is the real difficulty in attempts to stabilize prices on a product-by-product basis.

Another objection to commodity agreements is that they can only apply to a limited number of staple commodities; hence they only benefit the countries where such production looms large. The ensuing inequality as between countries which are big producers and those which are not is all the more serious when price-fixing not only tends to eliminate fluctuations, but establishes a level above what the normal market would bear. In such a case the price comprises an element of aid which only the countries exporting that particular commodity enjoy, and which they receive irrespective of their real needs. The commodity agreements will at best limit the fall of prices for such primary products, while developing countries may also suffer from an increase in the prices of their industrial imports.

This all argues that, even if commodity agreements may contribute to reducing fluctuations in prices and changes in the "terms of trade," they must of necessity be supplemented by some more general device. Clearly, the problem of the terms of trade applies to more products and to more countries than can be helped by commodity agreements.

The basis of a general solution would be to agree that economic aid as a whole should be increased when the terms of trade vary to the detriment of primary products. It can be readily demonstrated that such a change means an advantage for the developed countries *as a group*, gained at the expense of the developing countries *as a group*. Each advanced country experiences a change in its terms of trade in relation both to other advanced and to less advanced countries. The mutual gains and losses cancel out between the developed countries, so that the net balance is a loss—or, if the situation reverses itself, a gain—for the developing countries.

The gain for the developed countries represents an unearned increment, a windfall profit, unrelated to the efforts of the country which enjoys it. It would therefore be fair in principle to repay such windfalls.

In theory, whatever base year is chosen as the most representative, gains and losses arising from the terms of trade could be reasonably measured by re-estimating what the imports and exports of a country would be at the price levels of that base year. The difference between those calculated values and the current values of imports and exports would indicate the gains or losses in absolute terms.

However, the statistical difficulties involved in such determination are almost unsurmountable. Thus it is not proposed to calculate in precise terms what the additional contribution of a particular country should be when it benefits from favorable terms of trade, or what deductions from its normal contribution it should be entitled to receive in the reverse case. But enough is known about the tendencies of industrial prices and of the prices of primary products to accept the principle that over-all aid could be either increased or decreased according as the ratio becomes more favorable or less favorable to the developing countries. It could also be a valuable element in sharing the burden of aid, since, by virtue of the structure of their imports and exports, the various developed countries are unequally sensitive to the fluctuations in the terms of trade.

It is not suggested that developing countries individually should receive *precisely* the equivalent of what they lose. They should be treated as a whole, with more funds becoming available in times when needs are greater.

To a considerable extent, this formula would ameliorate the difficulty, for a country with balance-of-payments trouble, in transferring aid abroad. Its share of aid would decline when its terms of trade deteriorated, but so would its balance-of-payments situation. As the prices for its exports rose, so would its contribution.

Also, the amounts of aid released would automatically be adjusted to the balance-of-payments requirements of the developing countries. The lower their own foreign receipts fall, and the more their external expenses increase because of price movements, the more financial help they need. Conversely, the less help they will need the more favorable terms of trade cause income and economic activity at home to increase and make more money available.

The recipient countries would be taught to manage their own affairs in such a way as to accumulate reserves and increase tax receipts designed to finance development when times are good; and they would receive more external aid for both development and balance-of-payment purposes when times were bad.

A world-wide financial mechanism of the kind suggested— reinforced by the agricultural plan discussed earlier (see pages 36-37)—could usefully supplement attempts to stabilize prices on a product-by-product basis.

Roughly speaking, a sum of around $7 billion is the maximum

annual gain or loss—based on an average reference year—that variations in terms of trade may cause to developing countries.

Each developed country would, of course, have to find its own ways for raising the amounts necessary to meet any increase in its aid contribution. Indirect taxation of imports or exports might absorb part of the price fluctuation and contribute to internal stability. To some extent, profits taxes would produce higher yields when the terms of trade improve, provided internal prices are more stable than import or export prices. The real problem is the extent to which a country has to balance its budget or allow itself a surplus or a deficit in the light of its general economic position.

As to distributing aid to the developing countries, it would not need to be governed by the specific variations in their terms of trade. The first test for aid should be a country s capacity for absorption, its ability to use the aid for development. The second test should be the gap between the requirements of investment and the internal savings which could go to meet them.

In brief, the need for capital can be affected by variations in the terms of trade. But every other aspect of the problem must also be taken into account, including the development of domestic savings and the level of foreign investments.

A system of such windfall repayment calls for no special sacrifice on the part of any country, apart from relinquishing gains that have not been genuinely earned but gained at the expense of the poorest countries. It complements the earlier proposals for distribution of food supplies.

To the extent that the reconstruction of the world market in agricultural products raises prices, the contribution of the countries benefiting from such a rise would be greater, and that of the countries adversely affected by it would be reduced.

It is at once the most appropriate, politically speaking the most convincing, response to a justified claim—and in the precise degree to which the claim *is* justified.

5 RULES OF FAIR COMPETITION

THE GOAL: To find fair rules of competition which will remove such barriers to freer trade as the "dumping" of surplus goods, cartels which divide markets or fix prices, export subsidies and other distortions of markets.

ON SEPTEMBER 26, 1962, eight American steel companies complained to the Treasury—under the antidumping law of 1921—that hot-rolled carbon-steel wire rods from West Germany, Belgium, Luxembourg, France and Japan were being sold in the United States at less than fair value.

In April, 1963, as American investigations of this alleged dumping were in process, German newspapers were complaining that the German market has been repeatedly disturbed by low-priced American products, claiming that polyethylene has been sold at prices 40 percent below the United States domestic level, lead and zinc products at 30 percent below.

These two incidents demonstrate that the lowering of trade barriers between the United States and Europe will have to be accompanied by some effective rules of competition, to be applied to the activities of both firms and governments. If freer trade is to succeed, such rules of competition must apply especially to fair methods of determining prices. To be fair, prices should not be distorted by dumping, by cartels or by abnormal government subsidies.

52

What rules are needed in the matter of dumping?

The General Agreement on Trade and Tariffs (GATT) defines dumping and lays down a procedure for dealing with it. But in view of the number of cases which continue to disturb international trade, and the long delays in settling them, it is doubtful if either the definition or the procedure is satisfactory.

Dumping exists, says GATT, if sales are made at prices which (1) are lower than those charged by the same firm in its domestic market, (2) differ as between various export markets, or (3) are lower than cost price. Any one of these criteria suffices to justify, on paper, a charge of dumping, and defensive measures, by governments concerned.

Two of these criteria, however, are very elusive. Whether a given price is below cost is as difficult to determine as the cost prices of a foreign producer, and even more difficult to prove. Whether different prices are charged in different markets presumes that such transactions are known, which is unlikely, and even if they were known, the transactions would have to be exactly comparable for discrimination to be shown. In actual practice, only the first criterion can ever be applied: comparing the export sale price with the domestic market price. Even then account must be taken of indirect taxes which, applying only to the internal market, make exports that much cheaper. But comparison is at least feasible, though it is a much stricter definition of dumping than the definition of price discrimination on the home market.

In applying this criterion GATT's practice seems to be somewhat confusing:

• It leaves the door wide-open to governments to take defensive measures at the request of their own industries, when these suffer or fear damage.

• The door is half-closed again by the fact that the contracting parties agree that action should be limited to cases where dumping results in substantial injury, such as closing down of businesses, unemployment or serious financial constraints. Defensive measures can thus be challenged if injury is not proved. The governments then negotiate and, if they disagree, submit their dispute for arbitration by GATT.

Clearly, it would seem better to find a criterion of dumping which could be applied more quickly, logically and effectively. As international relations grow closer, there would be great advantage in aligning the idea of dumping to the definitions of price discrimination applying on the home market.

The United States' concept of such discrimination is that it exists if a firm applies different prices to like transactions, except to meet competition. Virtually the same idea is applied by the treaty which established the European Coal and Steel Community (the Common Market's treaty is less specific, and leaves it to detailed regulations to implement the general principle laid down).

What would be the effects of applying this concept of discrimination to international trade?

Since prices may be cut to meet competition, it would unquestionably allow sales at prices below those of the exporter's domestic market. However, it would prevent any substantial injury, since the *undercutting* of prices would not be involved, but merely the *aligning* of prices to those of the foreign market. Using the system applicable to the domestic market should reconcile the contradictions of the present methods.

But what, someone may object, if a foreign business creates a fictitious competitor whose price scales justify the lower prices he intends to apply? Such maneuvers can easily be thwarted, since only a small amount of vigilance is needed to detect "competitors" who are little more than an office, a telephone and a sample case.

But what—and this is a more difficult question—if the price of a given product, say, is $4 in Japan, $5 in America, and $6 in Europe, and Japan is selling it in the States at $4.50, above its own domestic price but well below both the others? Doubtless the European exporter would claim the right to meet this competition by also underselling the American domestic price, contending that the price level in question was already in existence and no additional injury could occur by other sellers following suit. But in this case it must be recognized that the *volume* of sales is a relevant consideration.

That is so because modest sales by a well-placed producer could have only a limited effect, while mass sales by other suppliers could be very disruptive. Therefore, the arbitration procedures should accent adjustment to domestic prices but not to those of other foreign exporters.

The rules would be easily applied to standard, identical products such as steel I-beams or cold-rolled sheets. But what of articles with brand names and model numbers—for example, a Volkswagen automobile? How is the proper relation of a Volkswagen's price to that of, say, a Swedish Volvo to be determined? It is possible to establish a fairly reliable price scale for a certain range of models produced by different firms, particularly if alternative export markets can be compared to test the scale's accuracy. The presumption, therefore, would be that dumping exists if a branded product is sold below its internal sales price *unless* whatever discount is offered is merely to give that product its *normal* place in the price scale of the market it is seeking to enter.

Such a concept is flexible enough to allow businesses to absorb part of transport costs and of customs duties in order to compete effectively. The limiting factor is the prospect of loss, or at least lack of profit, which might result. Within those limits, a manufacturer could assume as large a part of such costs as he was prepared to accept. That would not be dumping, as it is under present concepts.

Furthermore, under present procedures, the measures applied in cases of real or fancied dumping no more conform with the spirit of free trade than do the definitions of dumping discussed earlier.

Essentially, these measures are simply unilateral action, decided on by the government which considers its producers to be harmed, and take the form of additional duties, or compensatory levies, slapped on the offending product.

Of course, the exporter's government may then seek to have these levies withdrawn or modified, and if arbitration by GATT ensues, an unofficial group of experts will be appointed, whose verdict is almost invariably ratified by the contracting parties, including the disputants. The only trouble is, as much as a year may go by before a case is decided. In the interim, the right to resort to defensive measures can be used as an alibi to keep goods in storage—a costly procedure to the exporter— and prevent their release during the whole period through which competition may be considered harmful. The old rule, "Justice delayed is justice denied," applies sharply to trade. The Rome Treaty attaches prime importance to preventing dumping, as well as defensive measures that are arbitrary. The principle of increased freedom of trade has proved acceptable to the Community's members because it does not lead to such forms of economic warfare.

For the Atlantic Partnership, institutions of the Community type cannot be imitated in a context which is both wider and looser. But the procedure should be objective and expeditious. In order to reassure both importing and exporting countries, it would seem right in theory to eliminate both unilateral action and intergovernmental negotiations, and resort directly to an authority for arbitration.

The place for such an authority is clearly within GATT, for two reasons. First, GATT already provides arbitration procedures, so the partnership should not establish conflicting ones. Second, arbitration decisions will unavoidably involve other countries. Therefore the arbitration procedures currently in use in GATT should be given more official status, with provisions for them to be invoked directly by the importing country which believes itself injured by dumping. Such a country could meanwhile take emergency defensive measures, but should withdraw them immediately if the arbitrators found them unjustified. A brake could be put on the arbitrary use of such measures by requiring the importer's country to pay any losses sustained through their use if they were later found unjustified.

Just as we have sought to bring the international definition of dumping into line with the concept of domestic discrimination, so must we also aim at narrowing the gap between the rules applied to domestic cartels and those applied to export cartels. Both in the United States and in the Common Market the situation as regards export cartels is unclear. They are condemned only to the extent that they affect competition at home. But as trade barriers fall, there is only a difference of degree between home markets and international ones. Free competition cannot come into play if one partner or the other allows market-sharing or price-fixing agreements by its producers. Market-sharing is the greater evil, since it could set at naught the benefits that free trade should produce. Price-fixing works its chief evil in raising the costs for consumer industries.

(Incidentally, it is sometimes said that cartel agreements in Europe are only poor substitutes for mergers, to make up for the difference in size which puts European industries at a disadvantage with American ones. As the Common Market becomes more integrated, the tendency toward bigger concentrations is increasing—a trend which should diminish both the difference and the cartel-justifying alibi.)

The whole cartel field should be carefully discussed by the two major partners. The Coal and Steel Community, which allows cartels for exports, has rules which resemble America's. The Common Market has so far only provided itself with the instruments for a policy and has not yet created a body of precedents; in brief, all agreements must be officially declared, and will stand unless disapproved by the Commission. This system of compulsory declaration will take a long time to have an effect. Therefore discussions by the partners can be all the more useful, since an overlap already exists between the growing number of American firms in Europe and, to a lesser extent, the spread of European businesses in the United States. This trend is a potent argument for the elimination of discrepancies.

In passing, we must pay heed to the American fear of unfair

discrimination by the presence of nationalized industries in important sections of the European economy—railroads, telephone, power, etc. In fact, these are usually run on lines similar to private concerns, and efforts to make them pay their way cause them to buy their supplies as cheaply as possible, regardless of the supplier's nationality. The rules of the Common Market already forbid such industries from exercising national favoritism as against another Common Market country.

The problem of purchases by governments themselves is more serious, although the "Buy American" Act makes favoritism at least as strong in the United States as in Europe. More important are military contracts, which in all countries play the same role of helping industries whose competitive capacity is uncertain.

Preferential purchases by public authorities are a form of camouflaged subsidy. In actual fact, however, subsidies are chiefly important in agriculture, where they sometimes account for half the exporter's receipts. They have a disruptive effect on a country's own consumer industries, as in the case of subsidized American cotton, whose foreign users buy it cheaper than Americans themselves, and send it back in finished goods underselling America's own. Our proposals for re-establishing a world agricultural market, and a new balance of prices, aim at eliminating the need for such subsidies. All subsidies work counter to the elimination of trade barriers. The whole problem, however, requires deeper analysis. Such an analysis of the effects of subsidies within Europe occupied much of the preliminary work leading to the Rome Treaty, which required the gradual elimination of many of the internal subsidies set up immediately after the end of the war, though permitting such subsidies as those helping development in distressed areas.

The analysis that went on within the Common Market makes possible some general observations on the effects of different types of subsidy.

Effects of Various Subsidies

Subsidies which only benefit the consumers are relatively harmless. They act as one means of redistributing income, but they do not affect competition between producers within each industry. They may affect the relative development of various types of product by shifting demand, which is the inevitable effect of a redistribution of income. Apart from these, subsidies should only be contemplated when they tend to be self-eliminating by their own efficacy, like those assisting growth in the industrialized country's own underdeveloped areas. This assistance—like the tax-free plant sites which Mississippi provides to new industries—can be withdrawn when self-sustaining development is healthily under way. In the same spirit, temporary subsidies to deal with particular difficulties are preferable to permanent forms of protection. The best known, and most justified, are those to help industries and workers suffering dislocations from freer trade, to find better locations or better uses for their manpower and resources. Such subsidies are beneficial because they help defray the cost of change resulting from new competition, while at the same time making it possible to overcome resistance to change.

A more indirect form of subsidy is made up of export credits. For example, an American manufacturer may grant very liberal payment terms to get European firms to buy his goods in preference to others. The financing which such credits offer ends up, in conditions where price and quality are similar, by favoring imports over local purchases, thus creating *artificial trade* which would not otherwise exist. It would be incongruous to maintain such credits, in their present form, between industrialized countries which have decided to establish freer trade among themselves. They came into being in Europe when it had a balance-of-payments deficit, but have been kept on even after considerable surpluses have been attained. They are more a help to the exporting country, whose competitive position is thereby strengthened, than to importing countries.

In conditions of pure competition, credits and sales would be quite separate from each other. There would be an international medium-term credit market for customers who could get their credits wherever they were cheapest, to buy goods wherever these could be obtained on the most advantageous terms. This situation does not exist today; commercial credits are tied to sales themselves. Only a beginning toward international rule has been made: an agreement to limit the term of such credits to five years.

However, the European Community is already beginning a first attempt to make export credits multilateral—to set up a sort of credit pool from which the customer can buy goods in any Common Market country. But now that the European balances of payments show surpluses, the whole philosophy of credits should be re-examined.

The present system gives to financially powerful countries an advantage over their less developed competitors, and accordingly militates against a consistent policy of helping the development of others. The whole device should be progressively redirected to the simple aim of helping those countries which need foreign financial assistance. What is needed is a system of import credits which could be obtained either in the country granting them, in other countries sharing in providing such a credit pool, or even in less developed countries which have the technical capacity to produce the needed goods. Such a system would eliminate a serious cause of distortion in international trade, and would make a worthwhile contribution to the financing of development. This important reform illustrates what could be achieved by concerted policies aimed at expansion and a rational distribution of effort.

Distortions and "Harmonization"

As the Common Market began, much concern was voiced over the difficulty of "harmonizing" the uneven levels, in different countries, of wages, costs and other factors of competition which might give one member an advantage over another. The problem gave rise to a great deal of discussion, and frequently contradictory interpretations, of what constituted a "distortion" requiring "harmonizing."

It is now clear that all the elements which affect production costs, between various countries, can scarcely be equated beforehand as a condition of fair competition. It is, for example, clearly impossible to equalize wages when productivity is unequal. Indeed, as we have seen (page 13), it is on the very differences in the actual conditions of production that international trade depends.

The proper concern of harmonization is to correct those disparities in legislation or regulations which conceal, or even turn upside down, those differences in basic conditions on which trade has to be based. One example is whether social security payments—for unemployment insurance, old-age pensions, family allowances, etc.—are provided out of general taxes, as in Britain, or out of employer-employee payroll taxes, as in the Common Market. Therefore in a particular industry which employs a great deal of labor—as is the case in European coal mining—the whole burden of financing social benefits enters into cost on the continent, whereas it is partly shifted to other industries, through the tax system, in Britain. Another distortion which had to be dealt with at the beginning of the Community concerned the practice, in some countries, of paying women workers lower wages than men for the same work. For it is clear that if equal pay were not required for equal work everywhere within the Community, a special price advantage would accrue to those industries—such as the garment or women's gloves industries—employing large numbers of women and paying them less than male counterparts. A competitor employing large numbers of women at equal wages would have a severe disadvantage. The force of competition would quickly re-establish unequal pay everywhere. Hence the need, which the Community is requiring, to apply equal pay simultaneously in all countries of the Community.

The need would not be so great if even reduced tariff protection were to be maintained. Such protection could correct the inequality without any necessity for distinguishing between a distortion and the genuine, necessary differences in conditions of production. But the moment trade barriers were eliminated, the problems from such a distortion as unequal pay would become acute.

The Problem of Profits Taxes

Taxes on profits, whose rates vary from country to country, provide a particular example where the principle of harmonization can be applied very usefully. They represent a distortion which can have a major effect on which country a business may choose for new investment. Indeed, they may channel investment in the wrong direction, as the United States has been discovering. Because the 52 percent corporate tax rate in the United States is higher than some rates charged abroad, an undue incentive arose to invest in those countries where the rates were lower.

This is a problem which calls for an international harmonization of tax rates, because it cannot easily be solved by any country on its own. Such individual efforts move toward a deadlock of this nature:

• If a country applies two different systems of profits taxation, one for operations at home, another for operations abroad, capital needed at home may flow elsewhere.

• If it chooses identical taxation—as the Kennedy Administration sought to do to "bring the profits home" from overseas subsidiaries—its firms abroad will have a disadvantage against local firms with which they must compete. (Under such a proposal, the U.S. Treasury would claim the excess of the U.S. tax rate over the taxes paid abroad.)

The problem must be tackled on broader lines. We must recognize that the *freedom of movement* of capital is an important factor in channeling investments as the situation demands.

However, the proper *economic* direction of such movement can be entirely falsified by inequality in tax rates, because the range of profits after taxation may not be the same as profits before taxation. The last is the more relevant criterion for the economic allocation of investment.

This problem already confronts the Common Market, which, having adopted complete freedom of movement for capital as its ultimate aim, must find ways of harmonizing such inequalities.

It would be reasonable and desirable for the same subject to be dealt with in the Atlantic Partnership. It is one of the principal fields in which comparative study of the various systems may furnish valuable lessons. Harmonization which, by achieving comparable rates, allowed free movement of capital to play its proper role, would also solve some of the problems confronting individual governments.

Mutual, concerted action is all the more necessary since, in its absence, there is a danger of harmful rivalry by national financial authorities seeking to attract capital by special advantages. As in the case of male and female labor, the object is to avoid what could be considered an undesirable effect of competition: in one case, the reintroduction of wage inequalities to the detriment of female workers; in the other, the "erosion" of the tax system.

Two Worries: Differences in Size and Taxes

In the United States, concern is sometimes expressed at a supposed advantage which European competitors derive from a difference in tax systems.

In Europe, a similar concern is expressed at the supposed advantage which American competitors derive from the much larger size of their industries.

Both fears are largely based on misconceptions.

The federal government, in the United States, does draw most of its receipts from direct taxation of individuals and businesses. Such state or local sales taxes as exist are retail and have no effect on international trade. In contrast, European governments derive anywhere from one-third to three-fourths of their revenue from indirect taxes, either at each successive "turnover" or on the difference between the value of sales and purchases at each stage. Exports are exempt from such taxes whereas imports pay the same tax as domestic products. Thus European techniques allow considerable reductions in export prices, whereas fiscal charges are wholly included in United States prices. Nevertheless, it cannot be argued that the considerable use of indirect taxation in Europe results in any general competitive advantage. That is because taxes are simply a part of costs—like wages, the electric light bill or anything else—all of which may vary as between Europe and America. They are simply a part of the whole picture of the equilibrium of trade, a complex thing determined, not by any one of these factors, but by the interplay of commercial policy, movements of capital, the quantities of goods bought and sold and, finally, the rate of exchange. As we have already seen, the basic differences in the various factors of costs are precisely what create, rather than stifle, international trade.

However, the cause and effect of tax exemptions on exports, and compensatory taxes levied on imports, have been carefully analyzed in the Common Market. The analysis shows that it is the *different rate* of taxes on *different products* which makes them necessary, for if the rate were uniform it would be immaterial whether exports were exempted and imports taxed, or whether the rate of exchange were altered by a sufficient percentage to lower the export prices and raise the price of imports enough to re-establish the same price ratio.

As long as taxes vary from product to product, the lack of import taxes and export exemptions would cause serious distortions. Each country would import those items on which its indirect domestic tax was highest, and export those whose indirect tax was lowest. For example, if France taxed radio sets 33 percent and bicycles only 5 percent, whereas Germany taxed both at 10 percent, then the German consumer would find French bicycles cheaper than his own, and the French would find German radios cheaper than his own.

There are only two ways to avoid such distortions:

• Each country could give up differences in the rates applied to different products. This would work a hardship on lower-income families, since essential foodstuffs would bear the same tax rate as luxuries.

• Or the taxes and differentials could be the same in all countries trading with each other—equally low on foods, equally high on luxuries. This is only conceivable within a close-knit community.

A compromise solution envisaged in the Common Market is for all the member countries to have an identical tax rate—low enough not to work a hardship on essential foods—on all transactions before the wholesale stage. Each country would then be free to impose whatever additional taxes it desired on different products at wholesale or retail levels. Since, at the first stage, taxes in the country of origin and the country of destination would be identical, the export exemptions and import compensations could be abolished. Without such a single rate, frontier posts would still have to be maintained (to qualify exports for exemption and analyze compensatory taxes to imports) even after customs duties disappear.

European fears about the bigger size of American firms are grounded in fact: in most sectors, there are American concerns considerably larger than their European counterparts. Based on both population and per capita income, the American market is about eight times greater than that of the largest single European country—Germany. The Common Market is already, to an appreciable extent, enabling the size of European concerns to be increased; a tendency to concentration, regardless of frontiers, is steadily growing. Present-day disparities will thus tend to diminish. Nevertheless, the damage they could cause must be examined.

Europeans argue that a more powerful business can make

mistakes in the choice of its products or its models without endangering its very existence, whereas smaller firms may have to risk everything. Of course, there are certain spectacular cases—Ford's Edsel and General Dynamics' Convair 990— which show that the size of the losses may well correspond to the size of the business suffering them. In any case, what the United States market does indicate is that, in a large number of sectors, firms of very different sizes can compete with each other. Only certain sectors which require vast amounts of equipment, such as the auto industry, are merciless toward any but the largest competitors. (However, the main European firms have now reached a scale of production beyond which no great technical economies can be expected.) Even these sectors make use of a multitude of suppliers of all sizes. The important factor is not, normally, the size of the concern but the length of the production line. With few exceptions, the advantage of a large market is to permit strict specialization and standardization of products, without which businesses would inevitably become unmanageable.

The other European fear is financial, the advantage of the huge resources with which American firms can meet competition. Similar fears were felt by the French steel industry when the Schuman Plan for the Coal and Steel Community was first proposed—that they would be overwhelmed by superior German financial reserves. Actual practice proved the fears unjustified. French steelmakers demonstrated remarkable competitive capacity. Events proved that cost and selling prices are the decisive factors and that no amount of accumulated resources can withstand, for very long, a disadvantage in those crucial areas.

However, this fear is extended to the presumed ability of large foreign subsidiaries, drawing on such huge resources, to ignore profits while they build up their position in a particular market. In a protected market such tactics could indeed be used to gain a foothold. In a free market they quickly become impossible.

The moment trade is free, a foreign subsidiary which is taking little or no profits will soon find itself selling, not only to the market it wishes to invade, *but to its own market at home.* Its domestic consumers would prefer these low-priced, profitless goods to the profit markups at home. Thus there would be automatic correction of the differences in the price policies applied by a single international group to its products manufactured in different countries. The situation is similar to dumping, which would become impossible in a perfectly free market, since buyers would be free to purchase in any country where a particular group sold its products at the lowest price.

All this, then, becomes an argument *for* free trade, not against it.

6 GROWTH POLICIES AND THE BALANCE OF PAYMENTS

THE GOAL: *To create coordinated policies for economic stability and growth and for equilibrium of the balances of payments.*

FOR freer trade to be generally accepted and then maintained, two conditions of overriding importance must be met:
• Markets must be expanding.
• Each country must be in a position to meet the necessary payments to others.

Those two conditions are interrelated. A policy of expansion can be either prevented from starting or stopped once it has started by a balance-of-payment deficit. Under conditions of freer trade where there is such an interpenetration of markets, a policy of expansion can be stopped by the spread of a deflation originating elsewhere.

Thus growth policies must be coordinated as an essential condition for Atlantic Partnership. They are also one of a partnership's main objectives, since ever-increasing production is the only way to raise the standard of living as well as to meet those "many and burdensome tasks" which confront us, of which President Kennedy has spoken.

Freer trade brings more competition, but competition alone

leads to a higher volume of production only if there is fairly full employment. In such a case, competition brings about a more productive allocation of resources. If, on the contrary, full employment is not achieved, then freer trade may merely entail a displacement of workers, which, apart from its other harmful effects, is also a waste of resources.

At present the rate of growth among the domestic economies of Atlantic countries is uneven. Between 1950 and 1955 the rate of growth in the United States, the United Kingdom and the countries now comprising the Common Market was virtually parallel. After that, considerable divergences began.*

Expansion continued at almost the same rate as before in the Common Market countries. But in the United Kingdom and in the United States it slowed down, to such an extent that the low rate of growth became a topic of vigorous discussion in the 1960 American Presidential campaign.

The reasons for these uneven rates of growth are debatable.

It is always possible, of course, to grow faster from a lower starting point, and Europe's starting base, at World War II's end, was wide destruction of its prewar plant. And it is also true that faster growth results where it is possible to transfer underemployed people to more productive work, as from agriculture to industry. The Common Market countries, with 21 percent of their people in agriculture, have much more lee-way in such shifts than the United States, with only 8 percent so employed on farms, and still more leeway than the United Kingdom, with only 4 percent. Moreover, it is easier to absorb technical progress that has already been accomplished else-where—as in Europe's postwar use of new American machinery —than to open up entirely new techniques and territory.

The part played by services in the Gross National Product of a country grows as its economic development intensifies (in the United States, services now account for more than half the national product). A slowing of economic growth rate is

* See Table I, pages 114-115.

sometimes explained by the argument that productivity rises slower in services than in industrial production. But this view overlooks the fact that trade, transport and distribution are the decisive sector in services, and that their productivity can increase—if they are efficient—as fast as, if not faster than, in industry. For example, America's retail trade has shown great productivity increases through prepackaging of meats and bulk products, and through the spread of supermarkets. France's railroads have tremendously increased their productivity by greater efficiency derived from their postwar reconstruction. Americans may complain that their own railroads have poor productivity. But that merely demonstrates how much room there is for improvement.

In contrast with America's lagging rate of growth, Europe's own continued steady expansion is a striking phenomenon. The rate of expansion has not been the same from year to year, but, with rare exceptions in Belgium, there has never been any absolute drop in the Common Market countries' volume of production. There has always been some absolute rise, even if there have been reductions in the rate of growth in less favorable years. This continuity not only fosters a high *average* rate of growth, but also helps *maintain itself*, since the continuity of growth encourages more investment. The very high initial rate of expansion, based on reconstruction from the low starting points of postwar devastation, was faster than the rate which the Common Market has since maintained, but this does not diminish the decisive influence of economic integration created by the Common Market. On the contrary, the Common Market's efficiency is adequately proved by the *continuation* of rates of expansion not far below that earlier period, as compared with the distinct break in growth rhythm registered by the United States and the United Kingdom.

Both these countries have experienced drops which entail *absolute* reductions in their volume of production. Although these recessions have been moderate, and followed by rapid recovery, the average growth rate is less high than it would have been if progress had been steadier. Thus an essential feature of any growth policy in the United States and the United Kingdom would be more effective anticyclical policies.

The biggest obstacle to a consistent growth policy, in both countries, has been difficulties from balance of payments. This is particularly true in the United Kingdom, which seems to have difficulty in reconciling increased production with balancing its payments. And the outflow of gold caused by the over-all deficit in the United States' balance of payments— despite an export surplus—is a constant obstacle to policies designed to raise the level of employment and to stimulate the rate of growth.

The American balance of payments presents a structure almost without precedent. On what is called "current balance," the movement of goods, services and revenue from investments, it has never ceased to show a substantial surplus except in one year when it fell to zero. Yet total spending for military aid, development aid and private investment abroad, less long-term foreign investment in the United States, constitutes a flow of net payments abroad which exceed the surplus of current receipts, creating the over-all deficit. Thus the paradox: there is a surplus balance of goods and services, and a *growth* of net American assets abroad. But at the same time the deficit must be covered by payments in gold—diminishing the gold reserves —and by an increase in foreign claims on the dollar in short-term assets.

Moreover, in recent years, America's global deficit, measured in losses of gold and increases in these short-term dollar claims, has been higher than expected, due in part to the return flow of American capital to Canada after it stabilized its currency.

However, there is no simple solution to the problem. It is clear that a reduction in aid and in the export of capital would reduce the present surplus on current balances. This is particularly clear as regards aid because much of it is in the export of American foodstuffs and because "tied" loans must be spent on American supplies. To cut these expenditures would have only a small effect at the cost of important political disadvantages. But the general trend now seems to be leading fairly quickly toward a better equilibrium. The American deficit cannot continue to exist without large surpluses in Europe. Actually, the growth of reserves has greatly slowed down in Germany, Italy and now in France. Price increases in these countries in recent years have been much greater than in the United States, which means that Europe's exports, being costlier, will diminish in quantity, easing the burden of readjustment which the United States otherwise would have to bear.

The British balance of payments is the result of a complex cycle of trade. Normally, the United Kingdom maintains a surplus over the rest of the sterling area, which in turn normally has a surplus over the rest of the world. But the United Kingdom has a deficit in its trade with other areas, which it covers with its sterling area surplus, with the result that the sterling area builds balances in London.

The reverse side of this mechanism is that England, supplied with currency by the sterling area, must return it to the area countries to cover their payments outside it as soon as their own surplus disappears. Periodically, therefore, the United Kingdom has to resort to a deflationary policy—sometimes because its own expansion leads to an increase in imports and to a reduction in the goods available for export, and sometimes to offset the imbalances of other countries in the sterling area.

The Coordination of Economic Policies

As free trade and free movement of capital increase, the greater are the international repercussions of the methods used to encourage expansion or stop inflation. For that reason, the use of fiscal and budgetary measures, rather than the indirect ones of raising or lowering interest rates, is preferable as a means of achieving expansion without inflation. This is so because the requirements of domestic expansion and of international equilibrium may conflict. A lower rate of interest can facilitate capital investment and consequently raise the level of economic activity, but it will also cause an outflow of both national and foreign capital to countries where higher interest yields are available. Conversely, a country which fears inflation and has a surplus in its balance of payments will only aggravate the international situation if it raises interest rates as a brake, because the inflow of new foreign capital seeking the higher interest will increase the external surplus. Thus the interest rate policy should be viewed mainly in the light of its external effects.

In any case, a rate-of-interest policy cannot be effectively applied by each country unilaterally. Unless there is agreement and close cooperation between the main central banks, one policy may simply cancel out another, and all lose their effectiveness even if they do not produce results opposite from those intended.

It is no solution to the balance-of-payments problem simply to shift it, like a hot potato, from one currency to another, by causing short-term movements of capital which only help one country's foreign balance at the expense of others'.

Economic policies can be coordinated more easily if the position of each country's economy can be studied from every aspect, and a clearer picture be thus obtained of the diversity of instruments that can be used. To this end, the Common Market has obtained the agreement of all member countries to produce a "national economic budget" which, in effect, gives a breakdown of the components of that country's Gross National Product at a given time—production, exports, imports, consumption, public revenues and expenditures, savings, investment, etc. Compiled on the same data and on the same pattern, these breakdowns make it possible to adjust assessments—which are necessarily imperfect—and coordinate efforts in various fields. A similar exercise could profitably be carried out in the wider framework of the partnership, indeed by all members of the Common Market.

The Common Market has already adopted a far more ambitious enterprise, a program designed to lead to a 50 percent increase in the total production of member countries as a whole in the decade 1960-70. An undertaking of this kind may be approached in two different ways:

• An assessment of the conditions on which such an increase would depend, and of the difficulties that might impede it; or

• An attempt to define actual policies and investments which would enable the target to be reached.

The latter would encounter resistance in some quarters, which regard even simple analytical forecasting as a first step toward "planned economies." So much misunderstanding has arisen over the economic plans adopted by some countries—such as *"le Plan"* which France adopted at the end of the war—that some facts will be useful to help dispel it. That is particularly true since this type of program is coming to be more and more widely adopted.

This is not to argue that general economic planning is necessary for a fast growth rate. Among the countries which have, since the war, shown the highest growth rates are Japan, the Soviet Union, Germany, Italy and France. France has established a regular plan for economic development, which, unlike the Soviet plan, is not compulsory. Japan has followed the French practice and Italy is about to start along the same line. Germany, on the other hand, remains strongly opposed to such planning. When you consider what those countries have in common which have had a rapid development, you find that, regardless of their political system or the methods which they have used, there existed a labor force which was unemployed, or inefficiently used, and that facilities existed to transfer it into more productive work. The method may have been coercion, as was the case in the Soviet Union, or it may have been the differentiation of wage scales, as in Italy, or the high level of invested profits which followed the influx of refugees in Germany, or, finally, the existence of a voluntary development plan, as was the case in France.

If France took the lead in adopting its method of economic planning, it was for two main reasons:

• First, some important sectors were state-controlled and represented a considerable percentage of total annual investment.

• Second, the government plays a large part in mobilizing short-term savings for the purpose of long-term investments—for instance, through the savings banks, which are state owned.

As a result, there was need to view such investments and such sources of funds within the framework of total requirements and of the demands of competition. What France did was to call on all the chief economic interests of the country —industry, unions, farmers, aided by independent experts and government officials—to help draw up *le Plan*.

This made it possible, from the first, to get far-reaching political decisions which might otherwise have been very troublesome—such as unions agreeing to work more than the required forty-hour week, and the priority given basic industrial investment over the construction of private housing.

Originally, the problem was simply to break the bottlenecks preventing general growth. Today, it is to reduce the uncertainties arising from numerous, and complex, possibilities of continued growth, by comparing the forecasts for the different sectors of the economy. This comparison, by giving each sector the assurance that its suppliers and customers are aiming at the same targets, makes for acceleration of growth. Government policy takes its place in the general scheme of things, making deliberate choices between consumer goods and the needs of the community—such as regional development, major public works and meeting the needs of wider education.

Coordination has proved possible also in other countries which do not use central planning. In some cases, the basic sectors were, as in Germany, in the hands of a small number of very big concerns whose plans, in effect, added up to an over-all one for the whole economy. In the United States, the publication of very detailed information about the position and development projects of the larger concerns enables the smaller ones to make reliable plans based upon these assured factors. An example is the sales and marketing plans that scores of

American firms were able to make in 1953 when General Motors announced a firm commitment to spend $1 billion on expansion that year. The "ripple" effect of such private plans on general expansion argues in favor of some pooling of the forecasts on which they are based.

In sum, the planning which has been successfully carried out in France, which is already being applied in Japan, and is now starting in Italy and Belgium has no other meaning than this:

It integrates government action within a general framework, and it helps to guide the action of all those concerned, without limiting their freedom or impinging on their initiative.

If the correct conclusions were to be drawn from these planning experiences, many fears would be dispelled and the efforts of the Common Market for its long-term expansion goal would be more strongly supported by governments and could therefore be more vigorously promoted.

Such efforts constitute the proper limit for attempts at international coordination of investments. There can be no question of *limiting or prohibiting* any investment, since everywhere shortages are a thing of the past.

However, the relative advantage of various investments could be clarified by providing managements with full, objective and detailed information on market and supply prospects. This should be done without distinction between national and foreign investors. In cases where a given foreign investor might enjoy special tax concessions, subsidies or other special incentives from his own government, negotiations might be necessary between governments or within the Common Market to prevent the rule of equal treatment from giving any particular investor an unfair advantage. But such discussions should concentrate, not on the *principle* of equal treatment, but on the conditions that might be necessary to make it fair as well as equal.

What should be the general aim of an international growth policy?

It is by no means certain that each country should seek to

achieve a like rate of growth. The common goal should simply be this:

To ensure that conditions obtain everywhere which permit the highest level of employment compatible with the readjustments which freer trade will make necessary in some industries.

If certain fundamental conditions are fulfilled, progress should normally be more rapid in countries or areas starting at a lower level, thus helping them to bridge the difference.

The Problem of Balancing the Payments

The expansion which takes place in one country is an important factor in the expansion which takes place in another country. Exports are for every country one of the truly dynamic elements of demand, and the mere fact of their existence testifies to the efficiency and productivity of an industry which can successfully compete in world markets.

It is not easy to foresee by how much trade will increase because of the lowering of tariffs. This involves the reaction of demand to reduced prices and the degree to which demand is prepared to shift from domestic to imported products, when the prices of the latter become more advantageous.

The certainty that foreign markets will not be closed is perhaps a more important factor in expanding trade than, even, the lowering of tariffs. Doubtless it is this certainty, more than anything else, which has caused the trade of the Common Market nations with each other to rise faster than their growth of production. The percentage increase of their exports to one another is three to five times higher than the production growth. It is this certainty which can stimulate the kind of commercial effort—the confidence to make and carry out big plans—which is necessary in the modern world if there is to be any substantial increase in sales.

It is still unclear what relation the development of freer trade will hold to the rate of growth in the economy of the partners. Very searching, if problematical, studies are needed to throw some light on it. Individual countries do not increase their imports at the same rate as their consumer incomes rise. From this follows an important consequence: comparable rates of economic growth in each country are not a necessary condition for maintaining a balance of trade at constantly rising levels; on the contrary, comparable rates of growth might be incompatible with such a balance.

This is the long-term aspect of equilibrium. There is also a short-term aspect. The freer trade becomes, the likelier become unpredictable and uncontrollable short-term zigzags in the pattern of trade—for example, a sudden increase in exports, followed by a sudden decrease.

All these things make more important the problem of the balance of payments and the need for monetary machinery to offset dangers of disequilibrium. As the problems vary, so can the solutions. The arsenal of economic and monetary devices exists precisely to offset the imbalances caused by unequal developments in trade.

A proper economic policy must pay heed to the many different circumstances which can lead to imbalances of payments.

• All deficits cannot be attributed to inflationary policies, to "poor housekeeping." They can arise accidentally, from a bad harvest, from an interruption of supplies through strikes or disasters.

• In the case of developing countries an excess of imports over exports of goods and services should be considered as normal inasmuch as the gap is filled by an inflow of long-term capital.

• Imbalance can also be brought about when countries with a persistent and continuing surplus refuse to grant credits abroad or revalue their currency (as Germany revalued two years ago) to raise their export prices, thus easing the imbalance.

• More important, circumstances may easily arise where a country increases its imports more than its sales abroad because it is experiencing a rate of growth more rapid than other countries. In this case its imbalance is actually a service to the others, which are likely to share in its expansion.

It would be contrary to a policy for balanced growth to deal with all deficits in the same manner. It would be contrary to such a policy systematically to shove the whole burden of adjustments on countries with a deficit. To do so would condemn them in all cases to deflation, which might spread to other countries.

The main answer, therefore, is that there must be a co-ordination of policies whereby the rates of expansion in different countries and the direction which such expansion takes, the movement of wages and prices together with the factors which affect them, and, finally, as a last resort, a change in the exchange rates—are all considered in the light of their respective interrelationships and are treated as matters of common concern. It should be emphasized that one aim of these proposals for joint action is that payments be not only more evenly balanced, but that they also be balanced at a higher level of economic activity and trade. Such should be the effect of a new commercial policy with regard to the developing countries, of a broadening of agricultural markets, and of a variation of the amounts of aid in conjunction with fluctuations in the so-called "terms of trade."

7 THE INTERNATIONAL MONETARY SYSTEM

THE GOAL: *To reinforce the stability of the international monetary system in a way which meets the requirements of growing economic activity and expanding trade.*

THE solution of monetary problems—particularly in the balance of payments—would be far advanced by the proposals already discussed for coordinating economic policies. The greater discrepancies and swings which are likely to develop as a result of freer trade raise the question of whether additional monetary machinery is needed on an international level to deal with them.

Financial crises, affecting the stability of some of the major currencies, have been recurring. All this makes it pertinent to examine the requirements which the international monetary system should meet, and the reforms which may be necessary to assure (1) a greater degree of stability and (2) a better adaptation to the growing demands of trade.

An analysis of the American and British balance of payments shows the system on which international payments rest. The central banks hold, in varying degrees, not only gold but also dollars or sterling as the means of settling their external payments. This is the system of the *gold exchange standard.**

* See Table VIII, page 124.

Many criticisms are leveled against it. The fact that a comparable system collapsed in the crisis of the Great Depression argues that it needs modernizing and improvement. However, its critics differ, both on the evils they blame it for and the remedies they advocate.

One group of critics argues that the system is dangerous because to the extent that it holds the currencies of deficit countries as reserves along with gold, this encourages "poor housekeeping" and inflation. They say it does this, in effect, by taking the money which the debtors should have paid to others and giving it back to them. Holding it as reserve instead of demanding gold for it gives the debtor, in effect, a credit. Instead, they say, the debtor should be tightening his belt; his payments abroad should require a corresponding reduction in the money in circulation at home as the individual buyers pay it into the central bank to get the necessary foreign exchange. But this is not done. On the contrary—the critics continue—the other central banks leave the assets thus acquired *on deposit in the debtor countries,* where they become assets on which a fivefold expansion of domestic credit can be based. In the meanwhile, France, for example, has created francs to give her own exporter in exchange for the dollars he has earned. A double pyramid of credit, based on the same assets, is dangerously inflationary—so runs the argument.

The argument weakens when one observes that at a time when the United States had a balance-of-payments surplus, one which seemed unshakable vis-à-vis the rest of the world, the same practice already existed of holding dollars as reserve, of not demanding gold, of creating credits both in America and in the exporting country. The alleged cause does not always produce the same effects.

Actually, it is questionable whether any country still preserves an exact ratio between its credit expansion and its gold reserves.

In the light of present circumstances, the criticism just discussed seems to argue that the United States should apply a deflationary policy. In a country where expansion is already slowing down, where unemployment reaches some 6 percent of the employable work force, it is doubtful if this "cure" is in the interest of America, much less of the world as a whole. The American balance-of-payments deficit must be seen in its true proportions: it is only 0.37 percent of the Gross National Product. *Surely sounder methods can be found for adjusting it than dragging the country and others with it into a recession.*

Furthermore, to one who condemns the system of holding foreign exchange as reserves, gold is the only approved means for international payment. But any increase in the quantity of gold available to the West depends mainly on Soviet sales and South African production. That is to say, the health of Western trade would depend on an area threatened by very serious racial conflicts and a country which, in its gold market transactions, does not ordinarily seek to facilitate the harmonious development of trade in the non-Communist world. If this were the only way out, the risk involved would be serious. Of course, the price of gold could be increased by devaluing the dollar. Gold's price would have to be doubled to offset the dollars others had been holding as reserves. In that case, countries which are not gold producers would have to ship twice as much goods for the same weight of gold, and the producer—and large holder—countries would receive a most unfair, unearned "windfall." When so many underprivileged countries have so many urgent needs, such "generosity" would be misdirected.

A more obvious weakness of the gold exchange standard is its instability. Central banks, with the powerful means available to them, can easily offset any erratic capital movements by private owners whose holdings represent only a small fraction of the foreign claims making up a balance-of-payments deficit. But the fact that such powerful central banks hold the bulk of the claims does not involve any commitment to hold them over any length of time. Should a central bank become worried about exchange risks or possible inconvertibility, and convert its claims into gold, its action would start a domino effect. It would create doubts as to the debtor country's ability to honor similar demands; a stampede could begin. Short-term claims against the Bank of England are thrice as big as its gold reserves, and dollar claims against the United States exceed its own gold stocks.

Hence, the *liquidity* which this system provides is bought at the cost of *stability*.

For the key-currency countries the advantage of easy credit, stemming from the willingness of other countries to hold a currency, is offset by the fear of withdrawal or sudden conversion. Far from being an *inflationary* instrument, the gold exchange standard restricts room for maneuvering of key-currency countries; it *restrains* policies for growth and full employment, as the United States is now demonstrating in its inability to do as much as it would like in these fields for fear of aggravating the dollar drain.

For all the talk about gold, the fact is that it is making up, from year to year, a diminishing proportion of reserves. Increases in total world reserves have been very irregular from year to year, and manifest no relationship with the volume of world trade.

In fact, they depend on the extent of the balance-of-payment deficits of two great commercial powers, the United States and Great Britain.

Such deficits occur either simultaneously or alternately. At times, the monetary system is required to support the imbalances of the sterling area and the dollar area at the same time; at others, short-term movements of capital simply shift the problem from one area to the other.

There is some debate on the extent to which a regular increase in liquidity is necessary for expansion and trade. ("Liquidity" is the total of internationally acceptable means of payments.)

Actually, no consistent correlation can be observed in the past between the volume of reserves and the level of international trade or of economic activity. As a matter of fact, the ratio of liquidity to actual trade was at its highest during the Great Depression, when trade almost came to a stop. Moreover, the effectiveness of a given level of reserves is increased by international clearing operations, on a multination basis, which cancel out all the debts except the net balances left over, which are all that actually have to be settled. This makes the available money go farther.

These facts are admitted and even emphasized by those who think that the present system can generate crises. They consider that such crises could be caused by an insufficient growth of reserves or—worse still—by their sudden contraction following a crisis of confidence with respect to the key currencies. Certainly, the problem exists and will be denied only by those who believe in the oversimplified theory that all countries need only set their own houses in order to end deficits and thus make increase of liquidity unnecessary.

The true role of liquidity is best understood in terms of a business firm's own economics. Income and outgo never correspond exactly; hence the need for cash—whether saved up from past profits or borrowed for a particular need. Moreover, such a firm can have no increase of production which does not require an increase in spending and this increase comes in advance of any increased receipts from sales. In the same way, an expansion of national economies, and of world trade in general, may require an increase in reserves or their more efficient use.

The International Monetary Arrangements

The job of the International Monetary Fund, created after the war to help maintain equilibrium, is to place at the disposal of its members the means to overcome temporary imbalances. Immediately after the war there was a general shortage of dollars; both the European and the developing countries were on the same footing in that respect. Now the problems are different and, in order to stabilize the monetary system, the means must be at hand to help the key currencies in case of need. This led to special arrangements, since the normal resources of the Fund are sufficient only to handle the problems of secondary currencies.

The 1961 Basle agreement among the central banks has made it possible to neutralize the effects of erratic movements of capital by taking the currency accruing to the others and relending it to the country affected by the flight. The ten largest financial powers—Belgium, Canada, France, Germany, Italy, Japan, Sweden, the United Kingdom, the United States and, on a special status, Switzerland—agreed in 1962 to provide credits, as and if required, to each other to overcome any disequilibrium which any one of them might suffer. The conditions for using these credits are discussed by the members of this "Club of Ten," outside the normal proceedings of the monetary fund. Still other arrangements have been negotiated by the United States with several European countries, whereby dollar funds are set up in return for the availability of their own currencies to use in intervening against any sudden raids on the dollar in exchange markets. Such arrangements are normally granted on a three-month basis. The immediate aim is to gain their renewal and eventual extension of their duration.

These complex arrangements, satisfactory as they may be to the experts responsible for handling them, fall short of creating a climate of understanding and confidence around the operation of the whole monetary system.

No doubt this is a field where changes have to be gradual, and where the earlier they are discussed, the more resistance they meet. There is no lack of suggestions about what should be done next. When plans are actually discussed, the tendency is for experts to emphasize the differences. We do not propose, at this stage, to offer any final solution, but rather to assess the problems, to show the relationship between the various formulae which have been discussed, and to chart the common purpose which emerges.

The Current Line of Thought

Two main facts clearly emerge:

• No monetary system can adjust itself to the requirements of international payments if the supply of new reserves is linked—as it now is—to the external deficits of two countries, the United States and the United Kingdom.

• The risk of collapse can only be avoided by concerted action by the monetary authorities of the countries which have an important position in the financial affairs of the world.

The United States is already contemplating steps to help cope with the first problem. It has announced its intention of keeping several foreign currencies as reserves when its balance of payments again shows a surplus. Such a course would have two effects: (1) widening the number of currencies used as reserves and (2) avoiding a shrinkage in total world reserves.

A shrinkage would be avoided for reasons that are clear enough. Should countries now holding a part of their reserves in dollars have their balance-of-payments surpluses turn into deficits, they would meet it either by shipping gold or by reducing their dollar balances. The world's total gold reserves, though some of it changed hands, would remain the same. But to the extent that dollars were paid back to the United States, the world reserves held in foreign exchange would be reduced by that much. However, if, instead, America took on the currency of other countries as part of its reserves, its reserves would increase without Europe's reserves being reduced by the same amount. Thus total liquidity would continue to expand.

All this is helpful, but it is not enough in itself. For unless other international agreements supplement such a step, this would spread both the advantages and risks of the policy to many countries—the advantage of easy credit, the risk of sudden withdrawal which could still precipitate a cumulative monetary crisis.

Moreover, if the United States alone were to choose which

currencies it would hold, the sheer size of such operations might make the European countries justifiably fear the impact on their economies. The switches from one currency to another could subject their policies to hard external pressure and give even more concern. In any case, the prime element of stability would still be lacking from this system.

If all the countries were willing to guarantee the value of foreign holdings, this would remove the temptation to convert currency reserves into gold, since currency holdings bear a small interest rate and gold pays no interest. Indeed, this device seems practical enough if applied to those currencies other than the pound and the dollar which in the future would begin to be used as reserves. But apparently American and British authorities view with great concern any guarantees which would cover extremely large holdings accumulated in the past.

There is such an implicit guarantee in the way in which the United States Treasury obtains other currencies from central banks: it exchanges them for dollars put at the disposal of those banks, but each party must repay the same currency which it has obtained. Thus the guarantee is limited to new commitments of the United States.

By analogy, it is understandable that the British Chancellor of the Exchequer, Reginald Maudling, should have suggested that guarantees could be given but should be limited to *new claims*. His suggestion provides that the countries assuming such new balances could deposit them within certain limits in a special account with the International Monetary Fund, where they would be guaranteed, but not withdrawn unless some other country deposited a like amount—probably by the country receiving this credit whenever its restored equilibrium enabled it to replace its own currency in the Fund by others earned in trade.

Although this limitation of guarantees to the *additional* holdings of key currencies by other countries is understandable, it may be doubted whether it actually meets the issue. The greater the accumulated mass of foreign claims—even old ones—the more a sudden run is to be feared. The flight might even extend to the foreign owners of long-term securities, which, in fact, through the stock market, are just as liquid as bank deposits or treasury bills. In any case, a comprehensive exchange guarantee could only be envisaged as part of a general and reciprocating agreement. If such a proposition were made by one country alone, it would lead to an opposite result from that which is desired: instead of giving reassurance, it would attract attention to the risks inherent in such a currency.

There is, however, an argument against a generalized exchange rate guarantee which is worthy of consideration. When a country devalues, its domestic prices do not immediately go up by the same percentage by which it has reduced the value of its own currency in terms of others. Thus if foreign creditors were entitled to an additional number of, say, French francs or United States dollars, to make up for the reduction in the external value of such currencies, they would gain increased purchasing power over the goods produced in the country which has devalued. In other words, they would not only avoid a loss; they would, in fact, enjoy a windfall gain. If an agreement could be reached on a reliable measurement of the increase in prices, it would be fair, in any case, to limit the guarantee to the increase in domestic prices if it is lower than the external depreciation of the currency.

A truly stable monetary system will require one vital requirement as a minimum: The main central banks must refrain from demanding a conversion of their holdings *without prior consultation and in the absence of an urgent need.*

Though there is no formal undertaking to that effect, it is implied in the gentleman's agreement which the Club of Ten has already made. It would have a profound effect if the same countries would agree, as Dr. Suardus Posthuma of the Netherlands has suggested, to work toward *uniform proportions* of gold and currency holdings in the composition of their reserves—each country holding the same percentage of gold, the same percentage of currencies. Such a uniform ratio would be equivalent to a *consolidation* of credits. This would not have to be done overnight. It could be done gradually as each country received net payments from other countries, and made net payments of its own to still others. Those small countries, like the Netherlands and Switzerland, which historically hold mainly gold, could be exempted in return for agreeing to sell gold for currency temporarily whenever this was needed to forestall "raids" and stabilize the gold market.

However, this is far from the present situation. Some countries hold practically nothing but gold; others keep anywhere from one-fourth to almost all of their reserves in foreign exchange.

Such a system might seem to minimize the importance of guaranteeing the value of currencies, since if one country devalued, the ensuing losses would be more equally distributed among the different countries. But that would be true only if each country held, in addition to a uniform proportion of currencies in relation to gold, a uniform proportion of *each* currency. That could be done only if each country distributed its holdings of individual currencies in proportion to the deficits of the countries whose currencies were to be held.

This would scarcely be good practice. It would be tantamount to automatic credit for every deficit country, increasing with the amount of its deficit. Since not all deficits are alike, all are not capable of being treated on the same basis. Their causes are different, and remedies must be worked out and negotiated from case to case.

If the losses of a country's devaluation had to be divided, a more equitable and effective agreement would be to divide them in proportion to the total reserves of each country. Even the country doing the devaluing would have to participate on the same basis.

However, such a solution would be hard to negotiate. A country which had managed its own assets with wisdom and prudence would have to defray the losses of others who had been less wise in choosing their reserve currencies.

In the context of the present world situation, the partnership in losses which would be assured by a perfectly uniform composition of reserves as between the various currencies can only be conceived in a much more limited group of countries. *Such solidarity would prevail among countries agreeing to manage their foreign exchange holdings—or part of them—jointly.* Joint management of this type would have a clear advantage over the bilateral dealings which are at present the chief element in currency support; most often they are kept secret, with the result that several countries may separately grant credits to another country without knowing exactly, except through leaks, what each of them is doing.

If two agreements were combined, one based on a common management of currency holdings and the other on a uniform percentage between gold and currency reserves, the result would be the same as if a certain number of countries created a common fund where part of their total reserves would be deposited or pledged.

Against such a deposit of fixed percentages of reserves as proposed by Professor Robert Triffin, numerous objections have been raised, which should now be examined.

Objection: It would supply automatic credit, which is unwise for the reasons already discussed—and inflationary to boot.

Answer: The only automatic feature would be that, as each member's reserves increased, he would increase his contribution to the pool in proportion. The granting of credits by a common organization should be entirely a matter of discretion. Except for very limited and short-lived interim finance, it should be used primarily for the restoration of balance-of-payments equilibrium, by methods worked out jointly between the deficit country and the countries which would supply collective help.

Objection: Countries would not be prompted to pay the required contributions because their credit rights, unlike those in the Monetary Fund, would not be fixed in strict relation to the size of the contribution.

Answer: With the idea of automatic credits discarded, it is contradictory to try to link contributions with drawing rights.

To so limit them would also limit the discretion needed for their most effective use.

Objection: Governments prefer fixed obligations to those which can increase as conditions change. They try to protect themselves against commitments which increase in proportion to their liquid assets.

Answer: Firm commitments are difficult to keep when liquid assets are dwindling. An adjustable system, which provides both increases and decreases in relation to assets, is less risky in the end.

Objection: A scale of contribution, based on the level of reserves, does not correspond to the true resources of a country, which are its wealth and its income.

Answer: This is irrelevant. Cash or bank balances kept by an individual hold no fixed ratio to his fortune or his earnings. Nevertheless they involve the granting of credit to others. In the same way, a country which holds gold or foreign exchange is, of its own choice, granting credits to others. This is simply a question of making a country aware of what it is actually doing, not a question of taxing it on a distorted basis. Furthermore, this contribution, of a percentage of the reserves, has its advantages—it earns interest, and may enjoy a guarantee.

We have seen the pros and cons to this idea of a Fund supplied by contributions calculated on a percentage of the reserves of each country, and varying with them. Is it practical to build a world monetary system upon it?

It is not practical to introduce it among as many countries as are represented in the International Monetary Fund. There are too many members, including some whose reserves cannot even be exactly ascertained. The schedule of contributions would have to be altered too profoundly. Some countries whose commitments are purely potential—their currencies remain idle, without being used for credit—would still be entitled to reimbursements. In any case, the crying need is not to meet the deficits of secondary or minor countries, or of developing areas, but to ensure the smooth working of an international monetary system which revolves around a few countries.

The Road Ahead

The choice before us is between creating a mechanism as among all the members of the Club of Ten on the one hand or, on the other, creating a system feasible for the Common Market to use in a partnership with the United States, in liaison with other countries.

Such a choice is inherent in the steps which Europe must take, in any event, in order to complete its unity. The Common Market Commission, in the program of action submitted to promote its future goals, points out that any change in the exchange rate of one of the European currencies—after the integration of markets has been completed, and common prices established through a common agricultural policy—would entail intolerable disruptions. It is true that exchange rate adjustments are not excluded in the transitional period while these integrations are taking place, and may remain necessary as one of the compensating factors in the new equilibrium which is being gradually established.

Nevertheless, this large fact stands out strikingly:

Full freedom in the movement of goods, capital and men is equivalent to full monetary convertibility.

And this even bigger fact emerges:

Full convertibility, with fixed exchange rates, requires exactly the same conditions as a single currency.

The only difference is that separate treasuries and currency denominations would be maintained. Convertibility at fixed rates constitutes *de facto* monetary union. The creation of a common currency, which would define monetary fusion, would only mean formal recognition of what had already come about.

Before this momentous event takes place, many other important requirements must be met simultaneously: a stabilization in price relations, toward which the Common Market by its very existence is working; the gearing of wage rates to productivity, which the Market also is gradually bringing about;

a reduction of differences between tax systems; and coordination of budget policies. Finally, the Market will need to coordinate credit policies to an extent which would not be very different from the operation of a federal reserve system.

These goals are all attainable and evolving. So is monetary union. Since it is both necessary and possible in the Common Market, it is only natural to think of it as the best framework for setting up a system in which member states might place an agreed portion of their reserves to be managed jointly. This portion could be increased. Thus the members would command permanent, institutionalized resources designed to aid one another's balances of payments, in case of difficulties, as provided by the Treaty of Rome. They would also have more opportunities to provide loans of a longer term to other countries, particularly in the developing areas. Indeed, they could lend more, and more confidently, because the balance of payments for the Common Market as a whole would be more stable than for any single member country, since the deficits of one toward the others would be canceled out by the corresponding surpluses within the group.

Such a mechanism, which has been proposed by the Commission, would gain tremendously in importance if it could embrace Great Britain as well. Under present conditions, Britain all by itself has to provide a counterweight for the whole sterling area. As a member of the group, its currency would be propped up by an imposing financial grouping.

Instead of bilateral relations between each country and the United States, it would be the responsibility of the group to deal with the American monetary authorities. This would also eliminate the danger of the United States alone deciding which European currency it should hold as reserves. As circumstances warranted, the partners would work out the rules on the composition of reserves on each side, and on the best ways of restoring balance in international payments.

To sum up, it may be difficult to establish a uniform ratio of exchange holdings to gold reserves on a world level—i.e., in practice between all the other countries which have a powerful financial position. It may also be difficult to agree on a general system of exchange rate guarantees, the need for which would not be eliminated by the uniform ratio. Instead, a scheme is proposed which is both immediately applicable and probably acceptable to all parties.

• To insure greater stability in the working of the monetary system, all countries would, on a world level, agree not to reduce the proportion of foreign exchange holdings in their total reserves provided such present holdings do not exceed 50 percent.

• Every country should be persuaded to join in an agreement whereby it would take its share of the losses caused by devaluation of its currency. The approximate formula might be the following: each country would agree in that case to reduce the value of its own reserves by the same percentage by which its own devaluation reduces the value of the reserves of all other countries.

Suppose, for instance, that there is devaluation of the United States dollar. The holdings of dollars for countries outside the United States represent about 25 percent of the combined reserves of the other countries. A 20 percent devaluation of the dollar would reduce the total value of such reserves by 5 percent. The United States would not pay the corresponding amount but would share the bill by way of distributing 5 percent of its own gold holdings to indemnify the other countries in proportion to their losses.

• To make the supply of reserves independent of erratic movements in the balance of payment of only two countries—the United States and the United Kingdom—both would agree when they had surpluses, to hold other currencies. This would prevent a contraction in world reserves when the external positions of these two countries reversed themselves.

• Such foreign exchange holdings by the United States, in particular, would, however, have the drawback of giving the United States Government a disproportionate influence, financially and perhaps politically, on the countries concerned if it were free to shift from one currency to another. Definite commitments should limit the risk, but it would be more effectively counteracted if the Common Market countries should establish a fund in which they would pool part of their foreign exchange holdings. This fund would, on their common behalf, negotiate with the United States Government the ratio of currency holdings to gold in the composition of reserves, and the form in which the United States would hold its short-term claims on European countries or on the Common Market as a whole.

• Such a fund is not only a necessary counterpart of foreign exchange holdings by the United States; it serves the essential purpose of preparing the monetary union—i.e., full convertibility at fixed rates, or even the monetary fusion, the creation of a single unit—which will be the necessity as well as the outcome of the Common Market once fully achieved.

Such a scheme would go a long way toward strengthening the monetary system of the West. It would extend the principle as well as the practice of partnership between equals from the economic field into monetary matters.

8 INSTITUTIONS

THE GOAL: *To devise the institutions necessary to form and initiate the concerted policies needed to master the partnership's interrelated problems, to provide continuity for the solution of new problems that arise and to exert a continuously stimulating effect on men's minds.*

Scope and Interdependence of Tasks

ARE the world's present institutions adequate, with new directions, to handle the multitude of new and complex problems which must be solved if a true Atlantic Partnership is to emerge? Or do the very newness and boldness of these concepts require more effective machinery?

Before discussing this question, let us review the problems that have emerged from the previous discussion, the aims to be achieved, the difficulties to be overcome. Tariff negotiations are vitally important, but to be fruitful they call for a set of conditions which can only be achieved by common action in many fields. The proposals for such action, made in this report, break with some conventional habits of thought. Yet reflection on the aims, and the difficulties they raise, should help both to clear up false problems and induce a creative effort to solve the real ones.

These suggestions are closely interrelated:

• A method of negotiation is proposed and criteria are suggested to assess the protective character of tariffs and at the same time measure the reciprocity of concessions.

• Inseparable from such a liberalization of trade, the definition of dumping and the procedures to police it must be brought into line with those governing discrimination in the home market.

• Agricultural trade will not develop without a policy which, while preferring the direct subsidy of incomes to price supports, also aims at re-establishing a genuine world market, capable of guiding production, redistributing outlets and progressively establishing a true economic level of prices. By replacing food aid-in-kind by monetary aid earmarked for food purchases in any market, such a policy would help banish hunger and speed up development.

• Markets for agricultural production must, moreover, be enlarged by a concerted commercial policy which allows growing industries in the developing countries to enjoy the benefits of reductions in customs duties under the most-favored-nation clause. So long as these countries have not emerged from their underprivileged position, reciprocal concessions would not be sought, but these countries may reasonably be asked—through limiting the increase of their exports to industrialized countries —to make their entrance into these markets a gradual one.

• These agricultural and commercial policies are indispensable ingredients in any development policy. But another necessary ingredient is the coordination of aid, to increase its efficiency and continuity, and to offset the advantages which industrialized countries often derive from rising industrial prices and falling commodity prices. These losses suffered by developing countries through the "terms of trade"—often exceeding the actual aid given to them—should be offset globally in a way which would supplement the effort of stabilizing prices product by product.

• Such coordination as well as anticyclical and growth policies are needed if the countries within the partnership are to be able to count on mutual assistance in temporary balance-of-payments difficulties.

• This payments problem requires new machinery to reconcile *stability* with the *liquidity* necessary for economic and trade expansion, and to forestall serious crises in the monetary system of the West. In the Common Market's progress toward monetary unity, it should move toward the establishment of a fund through which it will manage a proportion of member states' reserves—thus extending the partnership between Europe and the United States to the monetary sphere.

As one considers the interrelated unity of this policy, and the diversity of the fields it covers, two striking features emerge:

It is essential that the problems which are mutually interdependent be tackled jointly.

Yet the problems themselves are dispersed among institutions whose membership varies, and which are located in different cities, and even different continents. To wit:

• Commercial problems and labor problems are dealt with in Geneva by GATT and by the International Labor Organization.

• Agricultural problems are studied by the Food and Agriculture Organization, in Rome.

• Currency is the official concern of the International Monetary Fund, in Washington.

• Aid to the developing countries is dealt with by the International Bank in Washington and by the United Nations. However, it is also a function of the Organization for Economic Cooperation and Development, which meets in Paris, to discuss all these problems.

Since the OECD brings together the European countries and the United States and Canada, it may seem the logical focus for the policies we have outlined. In some ways, however, it is too broad and diffuse a machinery to permit the type of pinpoint focusing required. Let us examine the machinery in more detail.

At first limited to Europe as the Organization for European

Economic Cooperation—formed specifically to plan and direct the use of Marshall Plan aid—the Organization made a vital contribution to that job. It made an equally vital one to the abolition of the quota restrictions on imports between one European country and another—making this easier by establishing a multilateral payment system. Finally, in 1961, the two donor countries, Canada and the United States, after being very active observers, became full members.

In its larger form the Organization became a forum for discussing, not only the relations of the European Economic Community with other European countries, but all policy matters on which Europe and North America should reinforce each other. Today it comprises twenty countries and is widening— Spain's membership has been agreed to, Yugoslavia has been admitted as an observer and the entry of Japan is under discussion.

On the governing Council, *all* members are represented. Its deliberations are prepared by an Executive Committee. Other committees have been set up for different sectors: economic policy, long-term development, monetary problems, assistance to the developing countries. Both the executive and the other committees have a restricted membership: each of the big powers has a seat and there is a selection of smaller countries. In this structure each country is represented individually, rather than by economic groupings such as the Common Market. The Common Market governing body takes part in the work, but merely sits alongside of the representatives of the various member countries in a consultative capacity. This procedure does not sufficiently acknowledge the existence—or the interests—of the Community *as a unit,* any more than it does the European Free Trade Association, in which the United Kingdom and six partners are grouped. Between the numerous national delegations and a secretariat which acts only on their instructions, the responsibility for initiating policies, or maintaining their momentum once begun, does not fall expressly on any one.

An Immediate Tripartite Committee

If concerted action by Europe and the United States is to be developed in all its interrelated aspects, some concentration of both planning and execution is essential. In present circumstances—the impasse since Britain's rejection from the Common Market—the opportunities would be better explored if it were possible to set up, in a form that did not require treaty ratification, a tripartite committee embracing the United States, the European Economic Community and the United Kingdom. Each member would maintain liaison with the countries or groupings with which it has special relations—thus the United Kingdom would attend to the Commonwealth and the Free Trade Association members, and the Common Market to its members in Europe and associated countries in Africa.

This more flexible and manageable body would not supersede the OECD or GATT or any other organization of wide international scope. What it could do would be to prepare the *essentials* for tariff negotiations, to explore the different fields where action on a large scale is necessary and urgent and, finally, by this means to open the way again—perhaps faster than is now envisaged—for the United Kingdom's entry into the Common Market.

Machinery for a Bilateral Partnership

Only against that day when the partners are reduced to two is it possible to describe the bodies which should be responsible for concerning their actions and preparing their closer relations. When that day comes, it will not be possible merely to transplant the European Community's institutional setup to a larger scale.

To understand clearly why this is so, it is important to understand the nature of the Common Market's arrangements.

Alongside a Council of Ministers, on which the representatives of national governments sit as such, there is a Commission entrusted with a common responsibility to find and pursue the common interest.

The fundamental question involved is: what is the best, the most effective way of taking collective decisions affecting several countries?

A rule of unanimity would meet the responsibilities of an individual government jealous of its sovereignty, but this right of veto could also lead to paralysis.

A majority rule seems, at first glance, democratic enough— whether it means that each country has one vote, as in the United Nations, or whether the number of votes allotted to each country bears a definite proportion to its size, as in the Monetary Fund or the World Bank. But resemblance to majority rule in a democracy, where the mass of citizens decide within a single country, is more apparent than real. In the case of individual governments, defending what they regard as the national interests for which they are accountable, there is no guarantee that any majority represents anything but a coalition of interests, or the result of crude bargaining.

The solution worked out by the Common Market aims at a system of majority voting in which a high degree of objectivity is assured because the consent of the Common Market Commission is required and the Common Market Commission represents not individual countries but the Community as a whole. This is the actual, technical significance of "supranationality," which gave rise to much misunderstanding and heated debate when first proposed. It gives the Commission the authority to take decisions directly applying the provisions of the Rome Treaty—decisions that in domestic law would have the character of administrative regulations. The Council of Ministers votes by a weighted and qualified majority on the Commission's proposals, but can change them only by a unanimous vote. This, of course, practically requires agreement between both bodies since it is highly unlikely that unanimity can be achieved against the desire of the Commission and, obviously, the Commission cannot be forced to propose anything of which it disapproves. Thus this highly original system is based on a dialogue between the Common Market Council of Ministers, which represents the nations as such, and the Common Market Commission, which represents the European Community as a whole. This structure is completed by a Court for settling legal disputes and a Parliamentary Assembly which can by a two-thirds vote overthrow the Commission, but may also enter into discussion with the Council of Ministers, which always has the privilege of the floor.

Such a formula, which would involve a measure of effective power being conferred on a common body, cannot be transplanted to the Atlantic Partnership, since the United States is not prepared to yield such sovereignty. In any case, the scope and rules of the proposed partnership are profoundly different from those of the Common Market. In the Common Market a minority of members may disagree, but in a partnership of two equals there is no alternative to agreement by both if any effective action is to be taken.

Necessarily, the body to govern such a partnership must express, in its very structure, the relations to be established between the partners.

What are its requirements?

• It should bring together on an equal footing the U.S. on the one hand and an enlarged European Community on the other in a Council that would meet at a ministerial level.

• On the United States side, this would mean the heads of government departments or federal agencies. On the European side, representation would not have to be rigidly laid down. It would comprise, depending on circumstances, members of the Common Market Commission, ministers of national governments, or both at the same time. Nor should we exclude Europe's representation, at some future date, by members of an eventual federal government.

• The composition of delegations on both sides should depend on the nature of the questions to be discussed. The diversity of the problems calls for a similar diversity of representation. In any case, it would be important to keep the number of representatives small.

If there is to be unity of concept, and continuity of action, independent proposals must be made by a prestigious source, this performing, on an Atlantic scale, one of the most important functions presently performed in Europe by the Commissions of the Common Market, the Coal and Steel Community and Euratom. Since it is impossible to delegate sovereignty, it would seem advisable to set up, on a permanent basis, a group of three or four "Wise Men"—outstanding public figures distinguished for their impartiality, imagination and experience, whose moral influence would make up for what they lacked in delegated authority.

The Wise Men's responsibility would be to give continuous attention to the most pressing problems of the moment, and to make proposals concerning them which would be automatically placed on the agenda of the Council for its next session. The Council would then be required to accept or reject these proposals. Experience shows that merely putting such proposals on the table for discussion definitely would tend to stimulate action and facilitate agreement.

Since that is so, it would be desirable to set up the group of Wise Men as soon as the interim tripartite committee, envisaged earlier, comprising the United States, the United Kingdom, and the Common Market, has been established.

After the United Kingdom is in the Common Market and the partnership proper between the United States and Europe is formed and the Council created, the likelihood of effective action would be increased by the further creation of a joint Parliamentary Assembly. A European Parliamentary Assembly, chosen by the Parliaments of each of the member countries, already serves the European Communities (Coal and Steel, Common Market, Euratom). A similar group of members of the United States Congress could be chosen by their peers to meet regularly with such a group.

It does not appear advisable to create such a parliamentary body until the partnership has been established, since a parliamentary body can only function effectively when there is an executive with whose actions it can deal. Once the Council of Partnership has been created, a parliamentary body could stimulate the Council to action, discover its errors and compel discussion of its work. Such an Assembly would certainly make a point of finding out what action had been taken, or neglected, on the various proposals of the Wise Men. (Canada might well participate in the Partnership Council and in the joint Assembly if it were decided that one of the two partners did not consist of the United States alone but all of North America.)

It is clear, of course, that even institutions combining partners as powerful as North America and the Common Market will necessarily be limited in the final decisions they can take. They can decide only matters for which, in the first place, they have received delegated authority and which, in the second, are of exclusive concern to the two partners—since matters of wider concern will fall within the purview of existing international institutions.

Normally, the Council of Partnership will have to refer a matter to the bodies on both sides which have decision-making power. Above all, in the case of trade, monetary problems or even development assistance, agreements can only finally be concluded in the existing organizations, such as the Monetary Fund or GATT, where all the parties affected have their voice.

The Council of Partnership will not need its own secretariat beyond what is required merely to convene meetings and take the minutes. And its proceedings themselves could be prepared either by the OECD's own secretariat or by a mixed group of American and European civil servants.

Should the Council of Partnership be incorporated into the OECD? Probably not, since it would represent so overwhelming a force as to create the risk that countries not directly connected with either of the two partners might feel neglected.

Nor should the Council take the place of the OECD. Its function, rather, should be to act as a sort of motor, to pick up and convert to forward motion the initial energy provided by the Wise Men, who would constitute the self-starter of the machine, while the Joint Assembly would make the periodic "check-up."

Furthermore, instead of sitting alternately in Washington and in Brussels (capital of the Community), the Council should sit permanently in the city where the OECD is located (at present Paris). This is needed to provide constant liaison with the Organization, to avoid any overlap in preparatory work, and to make the best use of the existing OECD secretariat.

For a Broader and More Flexible OECD

One immediate benefit of this close association would be to give new vigor and greater flexibility to the Organization. Such flexibility has already been developing in the work of its committees, which, being responsible for various aspects of cooperation and development, do most of the Organization's real work. The OECD Council itself, containing all the member countries and deciding by unanimous vote, very rarely has to take actual decisions for the reason that matters are settled before they reach the stage where a single member can veto the action proposed.

This flexibility of committees was demonstrated in the case of Japan. Even before Japan applied for full membership in the OECD, it had already joined the Development Assistance Committee—one of the OECD working parties. It would seem equally reasonable for Japan, even before full membership, to join the Monetary Committee (No. 3), since it is already one of the ten countries (the so-called "Club of Ten") who at Vienna in 1961 agreed to supplement the resources of the Monetary Fund by making stand-by credits available up to a limit—$6 billion all told—for emergency stabilization operations.

If full use is made of precisely this kind of flexibility, the problem of the accession of new members to the Organization as a whole will solve itself.

It will come to be recognized that the *reality* of the Organization lies in its working committees, which bring together countries that have essential interests or influence in the particular problems that arise.

There is no reason why countries who do not belong either to Europe or to North America should not join on this functional basis. There is every reason why they should join.

This procedure would avoid a difficult problem. It is impossible, on the one hand, to close the list of OECD full members without appearing arbitrary and giving offense. On the other, full membership cannot be expanded indefinitely without making the Organization an unmanageable, impotent and veto-ridden mass. The more flexible system of participation in committees would ensure that each country could contribute, to its fullest ability, in defining and assisting common action. The important position of Canada—and also, probably, of Japan—would be recognized by giving both of them representation on all committees.

We shall thus have an organization systematically conceived as a *network* of committees, organized on a functional basis and served by a single secretariat. Such a body would prove an invaluable forum for the submission and wider discussion of the ideas of the two main partners before they are finally dealt with in the appropriate international bodies.

To sum up, a firm conception of the partnership between Europe and the United States should provide a genuine basis for creating those institutions which it needs for its expression, namely:

- A bipartite Council, helped by the proposals of
- Wise Men, outstanding, impartial, creative public figures.
- An Assembly, where representatives of the Congress and the European Assembly sit side by side, which would hold the Council accountable for its action or inaction on the Wise Men's, and other, proposals.

• For the immediate future, a committee of three—the United States, the European Community and the United Kingdom, aided from the outset by the Wise Men—should explore the paths of action to overcome the present difficulties. Around this nucleus should be built a larger gathering of the countries that will cooperate functionally according to their capacities.

Over and above its practical advantages, there is a deeper justification for a body of this kind.

The free world has no clearly defined frontiers, nor can it have if it is to maintain its appeal for all peoples, who are free and willing, to rally to it. Through the proposed "open door" policy which would be its most original feature, the Organization for Economic Cooperation and Development could measure up to the scope and the potentiality of the free world.

Illustrative Draft Agreement

The following draft is presented purely as an illustration of how the proposed Interim Committee could be created. Those who took part in the study are, of course, not committed to its specific provisions.

HENRY CABOT LODGE
Director-General

ARTICLE I

By the present agreement the participating governments establish among themselves an Interim Committee for Atlantic Partnership.

ARTICLE II

The aim of the Committee shall be: to eliminate the impediments to international trade, to concert policies toward underdeveloped countries, to promote a continuous and balanced economic expansion, to harmonize agricultural policies, to provide mutual protection against balance-of-payments crises, to adopt measures designed to prevent dumping, and, in general, to bring about a greater capacity for timely and effective common action. Signatories of this agreement shall accept these aims.

ARTICLE III

1. The achievement of the tasks entrusted to the Committee shall be promoted by a Citizens' Panel.
2. The Committee and Panel shall be assisted by the Secretary-General and Secretariat of the OECD, acting in a consultative capacity.

ARTICLE IV

The proposals of the Citizens' Panel shall be binding on governments unless a government shall within a period of thirty days expressly denounce the particular proposal.

(Comment: Thus the burden of effort will be on the government seeking to divide the community instead of being on the government which would unite the community, as has hitherto been the case.)

ARTICLE V

The Committee shall consist of three members as follows: the United States of America; the member states of the European Economic Community; and the United Kingdom and nations associated with her.

ARTICLE VI

The Committee shall work through the functional committees of OECD which may include representatives of any free world nation having a vital, direct and major interest in the subject under consideration.

ARTICLE VII

The Citizens' Panel shall be a small group of not more than five "Wise Men," who shall be persons of exceptional experience, eminence and independent judgment. They shall be public members, and not representatives of governments. In the first instance they shall be named by heads of governments, but, thereafter, they will choose their own successors. Their function is to exert a continuously stimulating effect by making proposals to the Committee, which proposals shall be inscribed on the agenda of the Committee and with which the Committee is required to deal.

ARTICLE VIII

The seat of the new Committee will be in Paris.

APPENDIX II. *Experts Participating in Studies*

Working Group on Economic and Monetary Policy

OSCAR ALTMAN—Assistant Director, Research Department, International Monetary Fund.

RAYMOND BERTRAND—Director of Payments, OECD.

EMILIO COLLADO—Vice President, Standard Oil Company of New Jersey.

JACK DOWNIE—Assistant Secretary General, OECD.

DR. OTMAR EMMINGER—Member of the Executive Committee of the Central Bank of the Federal Republic of Germany.

SIR ROBERT L. HALL, K.C.M.G.—Member of the Commonwealth Economic Committee.

WALTER D. SALANT—Consultant to the Secretary of the Treasury.

THE HON. ARTHUR M. STAMP—Managing Director, Maxwell Stamp Associates, Ltd.; former Director, European Department, International Monetary Fund.

CHARLES STEWART—U. S. Chamber of Commerce, Washington, D.C.

FRANK TAMAGNA—Professor at the American University, Washington, D.C.

JAMES TOBIN—Sterling Professor of Economics, Yale University.

ROBERT TRIFFIN—Professor of Economics, Yale University; former Economic Adviser to the President.

T. DE VRIES—Assistant Head of Department of Studies, Netherlands Bank.

Working Group on Trade Policy

MURRAY FORSYTH—Research Department, Political and Economic Planning, London.

BERTRAND DE JOUVENEL—Economist and writer, Paris.

JOHN PINDER—Economist Intelligence Unit, London.

111

HOWARD PIQUET—Chief Economist, the Library of Congress, Washington, D.C.

ERHARD POINCILLIT—Assistant Director (Trade), OECD, Paris.

MYER RASHISH—Economist, former Special Assistant to the President of the United States.

SVEN RENBORG—Director of the Economic Department, Council of Europe.

JEAN ROYER—Former Deputy Secretary General of GATT.

BERT SEIDMAN—European Representative of the AFL-CIO.

RENÉ SERGENT—Vice President of the French "Syndicat Général de la Construction Électrique," former Secretary General of the OEEC.

Working Group on Agriculture Policy

LOUIS H. BEAN—Agricultural Consultant, former Adviser to the U.S. Department of Agriculture.

J. T. BERESFORD—Agriculturalist, economist, United Kingdom.

COLIN CLARK—Professor, Agricultural Statistics Research Institute, Oxford.

DALE E. HATHAWAY—Professor at Michigan State University.

GALE JOHNSON—Professor at the University of Chicago.

E. M. H. LLOYD—Political and Economic Planning, London.

HANS AUGUST LUCKER—Member of the Federal German Parliament.

H. PRIEBE—Professor at the Wolfang Goethe University, Frankfurt am Main.

ROGER SAVARY—Secretary General, International Federation of Agricultural Producers.

M. J. WEST—The Economist Intelligence Unit, London.

MICHEL WOIMANT—Technical Adviser to the Ministry of Agriculture, Paris.

Working Group on Institutional Arrangements

PROF. G. L. BASSANI—Director of the Institute for the Study of International Politics, Milan.

ROBERT BOWIE—Professor, Director of Harvard Center for International Affairs.

G. H. BUITER—Secretary of the European Trades Union Committee, Brussels.

ÉTIENNE HIRSCH—Former President, Euratom Commission; former Commissioner General of the French Economic Planning Office.

STANLEY HOFFMANN—Professor of Government, Harvard University.

BEN MOORE—Associate Director of the Twentieth Century Fund, New York City.

ERIC STEIN—Professor at the University of Michigan.

"Rounding Up" Group

WILLIAM DIEBOLD—Senior Research Fellow, Council on Foreign Relations, New York City.

INNOCENZO GASPARINI—Professor of Political Economy, University of Venice.

ROBERT LEMAIGNEN—Former Member of the Commission of the European Economic Community, Brussels.

ANDREW SHONFIELD—Director of Studies, the Royal Institute of International Affairs, London.

SERGIO SIGLIENTI—Executive Director, International Monetary Fund.

LEONARD TENNYSON—Director, Information Services of the European Community, Washington, D.C.

List of Those Consulted Individually

AMBASSADOR W. R. BURGESS—Former United States Ambassador and Permanent Representative to the North Atlantic Treaty Organization and the OECD; Chairman, Atlantic Treaty Association.

CARLO BUSSI—Secretary General of the Italian section of the European Committee for Economic and Social Progress; Director of Statistical and Economic Services for FIAT, Turin.

RÉNE DUMONT—Professor at the Institute for Political Studies, Paris.

LORD GLADWYN—Former British Ambassador to Paris; Chairman of "Britain in Europe."

MANLIO ROSSI-DORIA—Professor of Agriculture, University of Naples.

U. W. KITZINGER—Nuffield College, Oxford University.

BARON VAN ZEELAND—Former Director General of the Bank for International Settlements, Basle.

The Atlantic Institute Staff

HENRY CABOT LODGE—Former United States Senator, Cabinet Member, Representative to United Nations.

PIERRI URI—Former Economic Adviser to the Common Market.

MARC ULLMANN—Formerly of the European Coal and Steel Community.

APPENDIX III. *Tables*

TABLE I

DATA ON ECONOMIC SITUATION IN 1960 AND ON GROWTH SINCE 1950

	U.S.	EEC	U.K.	OECD
Total population (in millions)	180,7	169	52,5	526,5
Population of working age (15 to 64) (in millions)	108,4	111,5	34,2	332
Employed population (in millions)	69,2	73,2	24,6	216
Employed population by sectors (in % of employed population)				
manufacturing	33	42	48	36
agriculture	9	21	4	20
services	58	37	48	44
Gross National Product (in billion dollars)	504	182	71	845 ª
Gross National Product per head (in dollars)	2,800	1,079	1,350	1,700 ª
Gross National Product per employed person (in dollars)	7,280	2,480	2,880	3,910
Rate of growth of Gross National Product (yearly average)				
1950–1955	4.2	6.1	2.6	4.5
1955–1960	2.3	5.1	2.6	3.0
1950–1960	3.3	5.6	2.6	3.8
Of which share of rate of growth due to increase of productivity	2.1	4.2	2.0	2.6
Investment in % of Gross National Product				
A. Total investment				
1950–1955	16.5	18.4	13.7	17.0
1955–1960	16.8	20.5	15.3	18.0
B. Of which residential construction				
1950–1955	4.5	4.1	3.2	4.3
1955–1960	4.6	4.9	2.9	4.5

ª Spain excluded.

114

Imports of goods and services			
(in billion dollars)			
1950	12,1	14,3[b]	9,4	46,5[a, b]
1955	13,4	25,5[b]	13,9	74,6[a, b]
1960	22,9	39,6[b]	17,3	102,5[a, b]
Exports of goods and services			
(in billion dollars)			
1950	13,8	13,6[b]	10,2	47,3[a]
1955	19,7	27,4[b]	13,4	76,0[a]
1960	26,7	42,8[b]	16,9	107,1[a]
Monetary reserves (in billion dollars)			
1950	22,8	3,1	3,3	32,8
1955	21,8	8,4	2,2	37,8
1960	17,8	15,1	3,2	44,1

[a] Spain excluded.
[b] Including intra-Community trade.
SOURCE: General statistics of OECD and information supplied by the secretariat of OECD.

TABLE II

SUMMARY OF TRADE
OF THE PARTNERS BETWEEN THEMSELVES AND WITH THE REST OF THE WORLD (1961)

	Manufactured Products and Miscel. (Cat. SITC 5, 6, 7, 8, 9)	Raw Materials (Cat. SITC 2, 3)	Agricultural Products (Cat. SITC 0, 1, 4)	Total (Cat. SITC 0 to 9)
	In Millions of Dollars			
U.S. exports (fob)				
To OECD	5.796	1.846	1.931	9.573
of which EEC	1.810	925	769	3.504
” United Kingdom	550	208	352	1.110
” Canada	2.700	485	378	3.563
To the rest of the world	7.553	1.705	1.798	11.056
Global exports	13.349	3.551	3.729	20.629
EEC exports (fob)				
(intra-Community trade excluded)				
To OECD	8.502	1.087	938	10.527
of which U.S.A.	1.928	105	181	2.214
” United Kingdom	1.182	246	344	1.772
To the rest of the world	8.528	632	900	10.060
Global exports	17.030	1.719	1.838	20.587
British exports (fob)				
To OECD	4.087	506	354	4.947
of which U.S.A.	610	39	141	790
” EEC	1.449	180	88	1.717
” EFTA	974	200	32	1.206
To the rest of the world	4.897	204	261	5.362
of which sterling area	3.264	81	192	3.537
Global exports	8.984	710	615	10.309
OECD exports (fob)				
To U.S.A.	4.549	1.493	895	6.937
To EEC (intra-Community trade excluded)	5.262	1.942	1.636	8.890
To United Kingdom	2.679	1.059	1.723	5.461
To the rest of the world	23.271	3.147	3.749	30.167
Imports from the rest of the world (cif)				
From OECD	5.805	13.157	8.825	27.787
of which U.S.A.	1.908	2.832	2.562	7.302
” EEC	2.013	5.940	2.839	10.792
” United Kingdom	1.008	2.829	2.285	6.122

SOURCE: OECD *Statistical Bulletins of Foreign Trade*, series B and C.

TABLE III

THE 80% CLAUSE OF THE TRADE EXPANSION ACT:
ITS EFFECT IN CASE OF BRITISH MEMBERSHIP IN THE COMMON MARKET

Groups of products (SITC*—3 digits) for which exports from the U.S.A. and the Six plus Britain amount to more than 80% of world exports (excluding intra-Community trade)	% of World Trade in 1960
533 Pigments, paints, varnishes, etc.	87
552 Beauty products, soap, cosmetics, perfume	89
599 Some chemicals	81
612 Manufactured leather goods, artificial leather, etc.	81
664 Glass	87
712 Agricultural machinery and equipment	83
715 Metalworking machines	82
716 Various kinds of industrial machinery	80
731 Rolling stock	82
732 Motor cars	90
733 Road vehicles other than cars	81
734 Aircraft	96
862 Photographic and cinematographic equipment	94
891 Musical instruments, record players and records	83
892 Printed matter	82

In 1960, the bulk of these products accounted for 14.8 billion dollars of exports from the U.S.A. and from the Six plus Britain, but it should be added that (a) exchanges of these goods between the U.S.A. and the Six plus Britain amounted to scarcely more than a billion dollars each way; and (b) some industrialized countries also export large quantities to the United States and the Six plus Britain, thus standing to profit from any important unilateral reduction of duties from these quarters. Such countries are:

Switzerland .... (approximately 260 million dollars in 1960)
Canada .... (" 250 " " ")
Sweden .... (" 160 " " ")
Austria .... (" 65 " " ")
Japan .... (" 65 " " ")
New Zealand .... (" 10 " " ")
Australia .... (" 7 " " ")

* SITC—Standard International Trade Classification.

TABLE IV-A

SUMMARY OF CERTAIN FLOWS OF TRADE OF AGRICULTURAL
TEMPERATE PRODUCTS (1961)

Importing Countries	Cereals (Div. SITC:04)		Dairy Products (Div. SITC:02-025)		Meat (Div. SITC:01)	
	Origin	Million $	Origin	Million $	Origin	Million $
United Kingdom	Total	592	Total	410	Total	858
	Canada	196	New Zeal.	166	Denmark	231
	U.S.	153	Denmark	87	New Zeal.	155
	Australia	67	Australia	50	Argentina	117
	U.S.S.R.	44			Australia	62
	France	25			Ireland	62
					Netherl.	59
EEC	Total	1140	Total	200	Total	382
	U.S.	400	EFTA	81	U.S.	56
	Canada	160	Switz.	29	Denmark	52
	New Zeal.	47	Denmark	33	Argentina	51
	Intra-Com.	177	Intra-Com.	107	Intra-Com.	150
	France	107	Netherl.	56	Netherl.	88
			France	31		
Of which Germany	Total	395	Total	109	Total	224
	Canada	97	Netherl.	37	Netherl.	57
	U.S.	96	Denmark	26	U.S.	48
	France	54	France	22	Denmark	38
					France	32
United States	Total[1]	59	Total	36	Total	375
	Canada	46	Italy	12	Australia	90
			Switz.	7	New Zeal.	56
			New Zeal.	4	Denmark	37
Japan	Total	330	Total	13	Total	14
	Canada	107	U.S.	9	New Zeal.	7
	U.S.	96	Netherl.	2	Australia	3
	Austr., N. Zeal.	50			Argentina	2

[1] These data are only shown for reference, since the U.S., far from being a net importer, is the largest cereal exporter in the world. To the exports which appear in the above table one should add those to Southeast Asia, Latin America and Africa, some of which result from commercial transactions and the bulk from aid programs.

TABLE IV-B

SUMMARY OF CERTAIN FLOWS OF TRADE OF AGRICULTURAL
TROPICAL PRODUCTS (1961)

Importing Countries	Coffee (Div. SITC:071)		Tea (Div. SITC:074)		Cocoa (Div. SITC:072)	
	Origin	*Million $*	*Origin*	*Million $*	*Origin*	*Million $*
United States	Total	970	Total	54	Total	179
	Brazil	368	Ceylon	22	Ghana	61
	Colombia	227	India	15	Nigeria	32
	Mexico	65	Indonesia	6	Brazil	26
EEC[1]	Total	509	Total[2]	16	Total	200
	Brazil	116	India	6	Ghana	57
	Colombia	54	Ceylon	6	Nigeria	33
	Africa	166			Netherl.	10
Of which Germany	Total	211	Total	10	Total	76
	Brazil	40	India	5	Ghana	34
	Colombia	39	Ceylon	2	Nigeria	14
	Salvador	37	Indonesia	2	Brazil	9
	East Afr.	25				
United Kingdom	Total	40	Total	323	Total	78
	East Afr.	15	India	175	Ghana	23
	Brazil	8	Ceylon	96	Nigeria	22
	Colombia	5	Rhod. Nyas.	11	Netherl.	13
			East Afr.	12	Brazil	9
Japan	Total	18	Total	3	Total	13
	U.S.	7	Ceylon	2	Netherl.	5
	Colombia	3			Ghana	4
	Brazil	3				

[1] Some member countries have special suppliers which do not appear in the global table. France, for instance, imports most of its coffee (70%) and its cocoa (95%) from former French Africa.

[2] Netherlands excluded=12 (unspecified origin).

SOURCE: *Commodity Trade Statistics,* UNO, 1963.

TABLE V

CALORIE AND PROTEIN CONTENT OF AVERAGE FOOD CONSUMPTION
OF CERTAIN COUNTRIES[1]

| | | Calories | Proteins | |
			Total	Animal Protein
Richer countries				
North America	Canada	3150	96	64
	United States	3130	93	66
Europe	Benelux	2930	87	47
	France	2940	98	52
	Germany	2890	78	46
	Netherlands	2970	80	45
	Norway	2980	82	49
	United Kingdom	3290	87	52
Latin America	Argentina	3040	95	52
	Uruguay	3110	100	65
Average countries				
Europe	Greece	2900	93	27
	Spain	2750	74	20
	Yugoslavia	2980	96	26
Middle East	Israel	2810	86	33
	Turkey	2850	90	15
Far East	Japan	2210	68	18
Latin America	Brazil	2500	62	20
	Paraguay	2500	68	26
Africa	South Africa	2580	73	30
Poorer countries				
Far East	India	2080	56	6
	Pakistan	1930	45	7
	Philippines	2010	50	14
Latin America	Colombia	2170	48	23
	Ecuador	2230	56	18
	Venezuela	2300	64	27
Africa	Morocco	2350	72	18
	Libya	2180	53	10

[1] In most cases the above figures apply to 1959.
SOURCE: FAO, 1961.

TABLE VI

THE FLOW OF LONG-TERM FINANCIAL RESOURCES TO DEVELOPING
COUNTRIES AND MULTILATERAL AGENCIES BY MAJOR CATEGORIES
1961 (Disbursements)

Donor Countries	*Grants and Grant-like Contributions*[1]	*Official Net Lending*[2]	*Total Official Flow*	*Total Private Flow*[3]	*Total Flow*
	In Millions of Dollars				
Belgium	107.4	−1.0	106.4	n.a.	n.a.
Canada	64.4	−3.4	61.0	n.a.	n.a.
France	880.1	72.6	952.7	311.8	1,264.5
Germany	169.2	404.4	573.6	210.9	784.5
Italy	47.2	21.0	68.2	165.5	233.7
Japan	80.4	151.2	231.6	144.5	376.1
Netherlands	69.8	−1.3	69.0	126.5	195.5
Portugal	11.2	18.6	31.5	n.a.	31.5
United Kingdom	248.0	199.0	445.0	(429.0)	(874.0)
United States	2,853.0	561.0	3,414.0	1,218.0	4,632.0
Total 10 countries	4,530.7	1,422.1	5,953.0	2,750.8[4]	8,703.8

Signs used: ( ): preliminary figure; n.a.: not available.

[1] Including grants, reparations, net loans repayable in recipients' currencies, net transfers of resources through sales for recipients' currencies, and grants and capital subscriptions to multilateral agencies.

[2] Including net official bilateral loans, net consolidation credits, and purchases of IBRD bonds, loans and participations, but excluding official loans for 5 years and less.

[3] Including direct investment, other new lending and private purchases of IBRD bonds, loans and participations; excluding private export credits for 5 years and less.

[4] Including DAC Secretariat estimates for net private investment for Belgium and Canada.

SOURCE: *Development Assistance Efforts and Policies in 1961*, OECD, Paris, 1962.

TABLE VII

COMPARISON BETWEEN UNITED STATES TARIFF AND COMMON EXTERNAL
TARIFF OF EEC—BRUSSELS CLASSIFICATION: 4 DIGITS—(1)

Products bearing duties of more than 25% (italics=over 40%)

Average U.S. Tariffs	Common External Tariff
Natural barium sulphate and carbonate (30%), Sulphites and thiosulphates (29)%, Compounds, organic and inorganic, of thorium, uranium or rare earth metals and mixtures of such compounds (30%), *Hydrocarbons (51%)*, Cyclic alcohols (38%), Halogenated, sulphonated, nitrated, or nitrosated deviates of phenols or phenol-alcohols (28%), Polyacids (35%), Amide-function compounds (28%), *Color lakes (54%)*, Propellent powders (30%), Pyrotechnic articles (28%), Matches (27%), Ferro-cerium and other pyrophoric alloys (40%), *Chemical products and flashlight materials (45%)*, Products of condensation, polycondensation and polyaddition (26%), Other artificial plastic materials (26%), Apparel and accessories (including gloves) of unhardened vulcanized rubber (35%), Apparel and accessories of leather (28%), Matting, straw bottle envelopes (34%), Basket work, wicker work (27%), Minofil, strip (30%), Yarn of man-made fibers (continuous), put up for retail sale (29%), *Woven fabric of continuous man-made fibers (48%)*, Wool or other animal hair, carded or combed (31%), Yarn of combed wool, not put up for retail sale (26%), *Woven fabrics of wool or fine animal hair (54%)*, Woven fabrics of horsehair (33%), Woven pile fabrics and chenille fabrics (28%), *Chenille yarn braid (42%)*, Tulle and other net fabrics, plain (39%), Felt and articles thereof (36%), Nets and netting of cordage (34%), Wicks (34%), Textile hose piping (32%), Knitted or crocheted fabric (31%), Gloves, not rubberized (33%), Stockings, not rubberized (29%), Undergarments, not rubberized (26%), Outer-garments, not rubberized (27%), Woman's, girl's, infant's undergarments (34%), Handkerchiefs (34%), Shawls, scarves (33%), *Gloves, mittens, stockings, socks (43%)*, Traveling rugs and blankets (33%), Bed, table, toilet, kitchen linen (32%), *Felt hat forms (80%)*, Headgear of felt (39%), Headgear, knitted, crocheted (36%), Artificial flowers (37%), Refractory goods (39%), Unglazed paving, hearth and wall tiles (26%), *Ceramic ware for industry and*	Medicaments (15—34%), Dextrius (22—26%), Carpets, rugs, carpeting, knotted (24—40%), Vehicles for passengers and goods (25—29%), Chassis (29%), Motorcycles (26%), Vacuum flasks (26%)

Average U.S. Tariffs	Common External Tariff

science (57%), Sanitary fittings, not of metal (30%), *Porcelain or china household ware* (52%), Household ware of other ceramic materials (30%), *Ceramic ornaments* (44%), Glass mirrors (34%), Household glassware (36%), Illuminating and signaling glassware (29%), Scientific glassware (26%), *Optical glass not optically worked* (50%), Glass beads (34%), Other articles made of glass (28%), Jewelry of precious metal (26%), Imitation jewelry (36%), Pins of iron or steel (26%), Iron or steel wool (33%),[1] Unwrought magnesium, waste and scrap (30%), Foil, powder and flake of tin (35%), Tungsten and articles thereof (32%), Interchangeable tools for hand tools (27%), Knives with cutting blades (27%), knife blades (28%), Razors and razor blades (26%), *Scissors and their blades* (50%), Clippers, cleavers (37%), Clasps, hooks, eyes (31%), Bells, gongs, non-electric (30%), Calendering machines (28%), Portable battery and magneto lamps (35%), Electric insulators (30%), Optical elements, unmounted (26%), Refracting telescopes (26%), Microscopes and diffraction apparatus, electron and proton (30%), Surveying instruments (34%), Balances (30%), Electro-medical apparatus and equipment (30%), Hydrometers, thermometers (39%), *Gas, electric and liquid meters* (41%), Revolution counters (42%), Pocket watches, wrist watches (35%), *Clocks* (58%), *Time clocks* (47%), *Time switches with clock and watch movement* (46%), Watch movements, assembled (38%), *Clock movements, assembled* (75%), Watch cases and parts (37%), Clock cases (26%), Watch and clock parts (32%), Other firearms (26%), Ammunition, bomb (29%), Dolls (36%), Other toys (34%), Christmas decorations (35%), Fishing and hunting equipment (27%), Buttons and button molds, studs (31%), *Fountain pens* (46%), *Mechanical lighters* (50%), Combs, hair-slides (28%), *Vacuum flasks* (49%).

[1] Plates, foil, powder, flakes of nickel (33%).

SOURCE: Committee for Economic Development, New York.

TABLE VIII

AMOUNT AND COMPOSITION OF MONETARY RESERVES
ON DECEMBER 31, 1962

	Total Amount	Of Which Gold	Of Which Currencies
	In Millions of Dollars		
North America			
United States[a]	16.156	16.057	99
Canada	2.547	708	1838
Common Market			
Belgium and Luxembourg	1.622	1.365	257
France	3.610	2.587	1023
Germany	6.447	3.679	2768
Italy	3.441	2.243	1198
Netherlands	1.743	1.581	162
United Kingdom[b]	2.810	2.600	210
Other Countries of the Sterling Area[b]	6.594[1]	1.080	5535[1]
Japan	1.842	289[2]	1432[2]
Sweden	753	181	573
Switzerland	2.872	2.667	205
Total	50.427	35.037	15300
Other Member Countries of the Monetary Fund	10.543[2]	4.218	6760[2]
Grand Total	60.970[2]	39.255	22060[2]

[a] The holdings in dollars of foreign government treasuries, central banks and other banking institutions amount to $16,902 million.

[b] The holdings in sterling of foreign treasuries, central banks and other banking institutions amount to $10,320 million.

[1] For Ghana, Libya and Crown Colonies, the figures are taken at March 30, 1962.

[2] Figures taken at September 30, 1962.

SOURCE: *International Financial Statistics*, April 1963.

125

GRAYSON KIRK	Columbia University
HENRY A. KISSINGER	Harvard Center of International Affairs
HANS KOHN	Department of History, City College of New York
EDGAR MCINNIS	Canadian Institute of International Affairs, Toronto
HANS MORGENTHAU	University of Chicago
LÉO MOULIN	Collège de l'Europe, Bruges
FRANK MUNK	Reed College, Oregon
ALFRED C. NEAL	Committee on Economic Development, New York
COMTE JACQUES PIRENNE	Historian, Brussels
JOHN SANNESS	Norsk Utenrikspolitisk Institut, Oslo
ULRICH SCHEUNER	Forschungsinstitut der deutschen Gesellschaft für auswärtigen Politik, Bonn
ROBERT STRAUSZ-HUPÉ	University of Pennsylvania Foreign Policy Research Institute, Philadelphia
GEORGE SCHWARZENBERGER	Institute of World Affairs, London
FRANK THISTLETHWAITE	University of East Anglia, Norwich
JAN TINBERGEN	Nederlandsch Economisch Institut, Rotterdam
MARIO TOSCANO	Historical Adviser to Ministero degli Affari Esteri, Rome
JACQUES VERNANT	Centre d'Études de Politique Étrangère, Paris
GIUSEPPE VEDOVATO	University of Rome
CHARLES VIDAL	CEPES Français, Paris
B. H. M. VLEKKE	Nederlandsch Genootschap voor Internationale Zaken, The Hague
JOHAN WILHJELM	Udenrigspolitiske Selskab, Copenhagen
KENNETH YOUNGER	Royal Institute of International Affairs, London